Achieving Excellence in Human Resource Management

Achieving Excellence in Human Resource Management

An Assessment of Human Resource Functions

Edward E. Lawler III and John W. Boudreau

Stanford Business Books, An Imprint of Stanford University Press

Stanford, California

Stanford University Press
Stanford, California
© 2009 by the Board of Trustees of the
Leland Stanford Junior University.

Printed in the United States of America on acid-free,
archival-quality paper.

Library of Congress Cataloging-in-Publication Data
Lawler, Edward E.
  Achieving excellence in human resource management : an
assessment of human resource functions / Edward E. Lawler,
III and John W. Boudreau.
       p. cm.
  "This is a report of the results from the Center for Effective
Organizations' (CEO) fifth national study of the human
resources (HR) function in large corporations"—Pref.
  Includes bibliographical references.
  ISBN 978-0-8047-6091-1 (pbk. : alk. paper)
  1. Personnel management. 2. Organizational effectiveness.
I. Boudreau, John W. II. University of Southern California.
Center for Effective Organizations. III. Title.
  HF5549.L2875 2009
  658.3'01—dc22   2008053117

Typeset by Classic Typography in 10½/14 Palatino

CONTENTS

TABLES AND EXHIBITS

TABLES

PREFACE   This is a report of the results from the Center for Effective Organizations' (CEO's) fifth national study of the human resources (HR) function in large corporations. Like the previous studies, it measured whether the HR function is changing and whether it is effective. All of our research studies have focused on whether the HR function is changing to become an effective strategic partner. The present study also analyzed how organizations can more effectively manage their human capital. It gathered data from many of the same corporations that we studied in 1995, 1998, 2001, and 2004. Thus it allows us to compare data from our earlier studies to data we collected in 2007.

We are deeply indebted to the Human Resource Planning Society for its support of all five of our studies. Thanks also go to the Institute for Corporate Productivity (i4cp) for its support of our 2007 survey.

We would also like to thank the Marshall School of Business of the University of Southern California for its continuing support of the activities of CEO. In addition, we would like to thank the corporate sponsors of CEO for their support of the Center and its mission; their support is vital to the overall success of the Center and is directly responsible for enabling us to do the kind of research reported here.

The Center has been and continues to be focused on doing research that improves how organizations are managed. During 2009, the Center will be celebrating its thirty-year anniversary.

Special thanks go to Susan Mohrman. She has made many contributions to this research effort. She and Ed did the first three surveys, and she worked with us on the fourth. She made major contributions to the design and conceptualization of this ongoing research project.

We would also like to thank Arienne McCracken and Lois Rosby for their help in preparing the manuscript.

THE AUTHORS

Edward E. Lawler III is Distinguished Professor of Business and director of the Center for Effective Organizations in the Marshall School of Business at the University of Southern California. He has been honored as a top contributor to the fields of organizational development, human resources management, organizational behavior, and compensation. He is the author of over 350 articles and forty-three books. His most recent books include *Achieving Strategic Excellence: An Assessment of Human Resource Organizations* (2006), *Built to Change* (2006), *The New American Workplace* (2006), *America at Work* (2006), and *Talent: Making People Your Competitive Advantage* (2008). For more information, visit http://www.edwardlawler.com and http://ceo-marshall.usc.edu.

John W. Boudreau, professor and research director at the Marshall School of Business and Center for Effective Organizations at the University of Southern California, is recognized worldwide for breakthrough research and consulting that bridges human capital, talent, and sustainable competitive advantage. A fellow of the National Academy of Human Resources, and formerly a professor at Cornell University, he has authored over fifty books and articles that have been translated into multiple languages, won research awards from the Academy of Management, and been featured in *Harvard Business Review, The Wall Street Journal, Fortune,* and *Business Week.* His latest works include *Investing in People* (2008) and *Beyond HR: The New Science of Human Capital* (2007). For more information, visit http://ceo-marshall.usc.edu.

Achieving Excellence in Human Resource Management

CHAPTER 1

What HR Can Do

Global competition, advances in information technology, new knowledge, offshoring, and a host of other changes are forcing organizations to constantly examine and reevaluate how they operate. Organizations are creating new strategic initiatives and significantly changing how they operate. They are utilizing new technologies, changing their structures, redesigning work, relocating their workforces, and improving work processes to respond to an increasingly demanding and global competitive environment. These important changes have significant implications for their human capital and their human resources functions. But are organizations changing their human capital management processes? Are they redesigning their HR functions?

During the past decade it has been difficult to find a management book or magazine that doesn't point out how many of the changes in the business world have made human capital—people—an organization's most important asset (Lawler 2008). The "war for talent" has been the focus of a great deal of writing focused on finding, motivating, and developing the "right talent" (Guthridge, Komm, and Lawson 2008).

The annual reports of many corporations argue that their human capital and intellectual property are their most important assets. In many organizations, compensation is one of the largest costs, if not the largest. In service organizations it often represents 70 to 80 percent of the total cost of doing business. Adding the costs of training and other human resources management activities to compensation costs, we can see that the human resources function often has responsibility for a large portion of an organization's total expenditures, and this portion is growing.

But the compensation cost of human capital is not the only, or even the most important, consideration. Even when compensation accounts for very little of the cost of doing business, human capital can have a significant impact on the performance of most organizations (Cascio 2000; Cascio and Boudreau 2008). In essence, without effective human capital, organizations are likely to have little or no revenue. Even the most automated production facilities require skilled, motivated employees to operate them. Knowledge work organizations depend on employees to develop, use, and manage their most important asset, knowledge. Thus, although the human capital of a company does not appear on the balance sheet of corporations, it represents an increasingly large percentage of many organizations' market valuation (Lev 2001; Huselid, Becker, and Beatty 2005).

Not all organizations can or should look upon their human capital as a major source of competitive advantage (Lawler 2008). In some organizations it may be sufficient to simply have talent that can and will do relatively simple jobs effectively. But in an increasing number of organizations, talent that is better trained, motivated, and organized can be a source of competitive advantage. It can make it possible for companies to be more innovative, develop superior products and customer knowledge, and offer superior services.

A growing body of evidence affirms that HR practices have a direct impact on the performance of an organization (for example, Ulrich, Brockbank, Johnson, Sandholtz, and Younger 2008). The initial work on the relationship between a firm's performance and its HR practices was conducted by Becker and Huselid (1998). In their study of 740 corporations, they found that firms with the greatest intensity of HR practices that reinforce performance had the highest market value per employee. They argued that HR practices are critical in determining the market value of a corporation, and that improvements in HR practices can lead to significant increases in the market value of corporations. They concluded that the best firms are able to achieve both operational and strategic excellence in their HR systems.

Roles of the Human Resources Organization

The HR function can add value by adopting a control-and-audit role. But two other roles that it can take on allow it to add greater value. Lawler (1995) has developed this line of thought by describing three roles HR can take on. The first is the familiar human resources management role (Exhibit 1.1).

The second is the role of business partner (Exhibit 1.2). It emphasizes developing systems and practices to ensure that a company's human resources have the needed competencies and motivation to perform effectively. In this approach, HR has a seat at the table when business issues are discussed and brings an HR perspective to these discussions. When it comes to designing HR systems and practices, this approach focuses on creating systems and practices that support the business strategy. HR measures the effectiveness of the human capital management practices and focuses on process improvements.

The business partner approach positions the HR function as a value-added part of an organization, so that it can contribute to business performance by effectively managing what is the most important capital of most organizations, their human capital. But this approach may not be one that enables the HR function to add the greatest value. By becoming a strategic partner (see Exhibit 1.3), HR has the potential to add more value.

AIMS	Support business.
	Provide HR services.
PROCESS	Build performance management capabilities.
	Develop managers: link competencies to job requirements and career development.
	Plan succession.
	Enhance organizational change capabilities.
	Build an organizationwide HR network.
PLANNING	HR (and all other functions) inspect business plans; inputs from HR may be inserted in the planning process.

Exhibit 1.1. HR management

AIMS	Line management owns human resources as a part of its role.
	HR is an integral member of management teams.
	Culture of the firm evolves to fit with strategy and vision.
PROCESS	Organize HR flexibly around the work to be done (programs and projects, outsourcing).
	Focus on the development of people and organizations (road maps, teams, organizational design).
	Leverage competencies, manage learning linkages; build organizational work, redesign capabilities.
PLANNING	An integral component of strategic and business planning by the management team.

Exhibit 1.2. Business partner

AIMS	HR is a major influence on business strategy.
	HR systems drive business performance.
PROCESS	Self-service for transactional work.
	Transactional work outsourced.
	Knowledge management.
	Focus on organization development.
	Change management.
	Human resource processes tied to business strategies.
PLANNING	HR is a key contributor to strategic planning and change management.

Exhibit 1.3. Strategic partner

In acting as a strategic partner, HR plays a role that includes helping the organization develop its strategy. Not only does HR have a seat at the strategy table, HR helps to set the table. Boudreau and Ramstad (2005a, 2005b, 2007) support this idea by suggesting that strategies can be shaped and enhanced by bringing a human capital decision science to HR's role in strategy.

In the knowledge economy, a firm's strategy must be closely linked to its talent. Thus the human resources function must be positioned and designed as a strategic partner that participates in both strategy formulation and implementation. Its expertise in attracting, retaining, developing, deploying, motivating, and organizing human capital is critical to both. Ideally, the HR function should be knowledgeable about the business and expert in organizational and work design issues so that it can help develop needed organizational capabilities and facilitate organizational change as new opportunities become available.

To be strategic partners, HR executives need an expert understanding of business strategy, organization design, and change management, and they need to know how integrated human resources practices and strategies can support organization designs and strategies. This role requires extending HR's focus beyond delivery of HR services and practices to a focus on the quality of decisions about organization design and human capital (Boudreau and Ramstad 2007).

As a strategic partner, HR can bring to the table a perspective that is often missing in discussions of business strategy and change—a knowledge of the human capital factors and the organizational changes that are critical in determining whether a strategy can be implemented. Many more strategies fail in execution rather than in their conception (Lawler and Worley 2006).

Despite compelling arguments supporting human resources management as a key strategic issue in most organizations, our research and that of others finds that human resource executives often are not strategic partners (Lawler 1995; Brockbank 1999; Lawler, Boudreau, and Mohrman 2006). All too often, the human resources function is largely an administrative function headed by individuals whose roles are focused on cost control and administrative activities (Ulrich 1997; Lawler and Mohrman 2003a; Boudreau and Ramstad 2005a). Missing almost entirely from the list of HR focuses are key organizational challenges such as improving productivity, increasing quality, facilitating mergers and acquisitions, managing knowledge, implementing change, developing business strategies, and improving the ability of the organization to execute strategies. Because organizations see these areas as important, the HR function is missing a great opportunity to add value.

There is some evidence that this situation is changing, and that the human resources function is beginning to redefine its role in order to increase the value it adds. The first four phases of the present study (in 1995, 1998, 2001, and 2004) found evidence of some change, but there was more desire for change than actual change (Lawler and Mohrman 2003a; Lawler, Boudreau, and Mohrman 2006). The purpose of the present study is to determine whether this is still true or if HR has turned the corner and become a strategic partner.

One possible view of the human resources function of the future is presented in a study of business process outsourcing by Lawler, Ulrich, Fitz-enz, and Madden (2004). It shows how four large corporations (British Petroleum, International Paper, Prudential, and Bank of America) transferred many HR administrative activities to the line, to outside vendors, and to highly efficient processing centers. The HR function was left to focus almost exclusively on business consulting and developing the organization and its human capital.

Outsourcing HR administration is consistent with Ulrich's argument that the HR function needs to be redesigned to operate as a business partner (Ulrich 1997; Ulrich, Losey, and Lake 1997). Recently, Ulrich and Brockbank (2005) have argued that the HR function needs to develop a compelling value proposition that focuses on how it can increase the value of an organization's intangible assets.

Boudreau and Ramstad (1997) note that the HR profession could mature in a way similar to finance and marketing. These functions also started as largely administrative units (accounting and sales), but have become business partners that help formulate business strategies and implement them. Indeed, they have been so successful in their transformations that they don't have to refer to themselves as business partners.

Creating Change

Describing the new role of the human resources department is only the first step in the HR function's transition to becoming a business partner. For decades, the human resources function has been organized and staffed to carry out administrative activities. Changing that role will require a different mix of activities and people. It will necessitate reconfiguring the HR function to support changing business strategies and organization designs. It also will require the employees in the HR function to have very different competencies than they traditionally have had (Ulrich, Brockbank, Johnson, Sandholtz, and Younger 2008).

It is clear that information technology (IT) will play a very important role in the future of the HR function (Lawler, Ulrich, Fitz-enz, and Madden 2004). With HR information technology, administrative tasks that traditionally have been performed by the HR function can be done by employees and managers on a self-service basis. Today's HR IT systems simplify and speed up HR activities such as salary administration, job posting and placement, address changes, family changes, and benefits administration; they can handle virtually every administrative HR task. What is more, these systems are available around the clock and can be accessed from virtually anywhere by anyone, thus making self-service possible, convenient, and efficient.

Perhaps the greatest value of HR IT systems will result from enabling the integration and analysis of the HR activities. They have the potential to make HR information much more accessible so that it can be used to guide strategy development and implementation. Metrics can easily be tracked and analyses performed that make it possible for organizations to develop and allocate their human capital more effectively (Boudreau and Ramstad 2007; Lawler, Levenson, and Boudreau 2004).

A strong case can be made that HR needs to develop much better metrics and analytics capabilities. Our previous four studies identified metrics as one of four characteristics that lead to HR's being a strategic partner. Managers and executives want measurement systems that enhance their decisions about human capital. All too often, however, HR focuses on the traditional paradigm of delivering HR services quickly, cheaply, and in ways that satisfy clients (Boudreau and Ramstad 1997, 2003).

HR has become more sophisticated in its measurement, yet this doesn't seem to be leading to increases in organizational effectiveness. Business leaders can now be held accountable for HR measures, such as turnover, employee attitudes, bench strength, and performance distributions; however, this is not the same as creating an effective organization. The issue is how to use HR measures to make a true strategic difference in the organization.

Boudreau and Ramstad (2007) have identified four critical components of a measurement system that drive strategic change and organizational effectiveness: logic, analysis, measures, and process. Though measures are essential, without the other three components they are destined to remain isolated from the true purpose of the HR measurement systems.

Boudreau and Ramstad have also proposed that HR can make great strides by learning how more mature and powerful decision sciences have evolved their measurement systems (Boudreau and Ramstad 1997). They identify three anchor points—efficiency, effectiveness, and impact—that connect decisions about resources such as money and customers to organizational effectiveness and that can similarly be used to understand HR measurement.

1. *Efficiency* asks, "What resources are used to produce our HR policies and practices?" Typical indicators of efficiency are cost-per-hire and time-to-fill vacancies.

2. *Effectiveness* asks, "How do our HR policies and practices affect the talent pools and organization structures to which they are directed?" Effectiveness refers to the effects of HR policies and practices on human capacity (a combination of capability, opportunity, and motivation) and the resulting "aligned actions" of the target talent pools.

3. *Impact* reflects the hardest question of the three. Impact asks, "How do differences in the quality or availability of different talent pools affect strategic success?" This question is a component of talent segmentation, just as for marketers a component of market segmentation asks, "How do differences in the buying behavior of different customer groups affect strategic success?"

Today's HR measurement systems largely reflect the question of efficiency, though there is some attention to effectiveness as well, through focusing on such things as turnover, attitudes, and bench strength (Gates 2004). Rarely do organizations consider impact (such as the relative effect of different talent pools on organizational effectiveness). More important, it is rare that HR measurement is specifically directed toward where it is most likely to have the greatest effect—on key talent. Attention to nonfinancial outcomes and sustainability also needs to be increased, and strategic HR can affect these as well (Boudreau and Ramstad 2005a).

The Emerging HR Decision Science

The majority of today's HR practices, benchmarks, and measures still reflect the traditional paradigm of excellence defined as delivering high-quality HR services in response to client needs. Even as the field advocates more "strategic" HR, it is often defined as delivering the HR services that are important to executive clients (leadership development, competency systems, board governance, and so on). This traditional service-delivery paradigm is fundamentally limited, because it assumes that clients know what they need. Market-based HR and accountability for business results are now recognized as important (Gubman 2004). However, these often amount merely to using marketing techniques or business results to assess the popularity of traditional HR services or their association with financial outcomes.

Fields such as finance have a different approach. They have augmented their service-delivery paradigm with a "decision science" paradigm that teaches clients the frameworks for making good choices. Significant improvements in HR decisions will be attained not by applying finance and accounting formulas to HR programs and processes but rather by learning how these fields evolved into the powerful, decision-support functions they are today. Their evolution provides a blueprint for what should be next for HR. The answer lies not just in benchmarking HR in other organizations but in evolving to be similar to more strategic functions such as finance and marketing.

In marketing, decision science enhances decisions about customers. In finance, decision science enhances decisions about money. In human capital, a decision science should enhance decisions about organization talent and decisions made both within and outside the HR function. Boudreau and Ramstad have labeled this emerging decision science *talentship,* because it focuses on decisions that improve the stewardship of the hidden and apparent talents of current and potential employees (Boudreau and Ramstad 2005a, 2007).

Organization Design

Organization design is increasingly being recognized as a key factor that enables organizations to develop capabilities and therefore to perform in ways that produce a competitive advantage. Organizations are adopting design features with an eye to the value they contribute—that is, how they help the organization accomplish its mission (Galbraith 2002).

Organization design is more than structure; it includes elements such as management processes, rewards, people systems, information systems, and work processes. These elements must fit with the strategy and with each other for an organization to perform effectively.

Organization designs involve complex trade-offs and contingencies. Clearly, one design approach does not fit all organizations. As new business models emerge, new approaches and organizational forms spring up to deal with the complex requirements that organizations must address. These new models include complex partnerships, globally integrated firms, customer-focused designs, and network organizations. Furthermore, multibusiness corporations are recognizing that different businesses exist in different markets and face varying requirements. Consequently, variation in organization design is increasing both within multibusiness corporations and between businesses (Galbraith 2002). Thus, for the organizations and the HR function, one size does not fit all situations. Different organizational forms require different HR contributions, and thus different HR functional designs and systems.

Contributing to effective organization design is a major domain in which the HR function has the opportunity to add strategic value (Lawler 2008). Increasingly, the only sustainable competitive advantage is the ability to organize effectively, respond to change, and manage well (Mohrman, Galbraith, Lawler, and associates 1998; Lawler and Worley

2006). Confirmation of this statement is provided by Lawler, Mohrman, and Benson's 2001 study of the Fortune 1000, which shows a significant relationship between firm financial performance and the adoption of new management practices designed to increase the capabilities of the firm.

Recently, O'Toole and Lawler (2006) have argued that three different approaches to managing talent have encouraged companies to look to human capital for competitive advantage. They represent different approaches to organizing and managing talent, and need to be supported by different organization designs and HR practices. For example, the low-cost-operator approach calls for an organization design that has highly structured jobs and excellent control systems. On the other hand, the high-involvement approach and the global-competitor approach require interesting, challenging jobs as well as flat structures that put people in contact with the external environment. Picking the right approach to management and then implementing it effectively represents a chance for the HR function to add significant value.

Design of the HR Function

All parts of organizations—operating units and staff functions alike—need to be designed to deliver high value. For staff groups, doing so requires the development of a business model—a value proposition defining what kind of value they will deliver that the company is willing to pay for because it enhances performance. It also requires them to determine how services can best be delivered.

The HR organization must think about whether the elements of the design of the HR function indeed do create a high-performance organization—that is, one capable of delivering maximum value while consuming the fewest possible resources. Doing so means concentrating on the way HR organizes to deliver routine transactions and services, traditional HR systems development and administration, and strategic business support.

HR must think about its own structure, competencies, customer linkages, competency development, management processes, rewards, and information technology to ensure that scarce resources are optimally deployed to deliver value. In addition to making sure the HR function is optimally designed, HR must also ensure that function adds value by helping design the company and its various business units.

In many respects it is useful to think of HR functions as multiple-product businesses. They have customers (the rest of the organization), products and services, revenue, and competitors (vendors and consulting firms). In order to exist they need to perform in a way that makes them the "best buy" in one or more areas.

Organization design decisions for HR functions as well as for companies as a whole are made in four key areas:

1. Which activities should be centralized and leveraged, and which should be decentralized in order to provide focus on the unique needs of different parts of the organization? The most efficient organizations are combining centralization and decentralization, trying to be big (coordinated) in functions such as purchasing, when there is an advantage to being big; and small (decentralized and flexible) in functions such as new product development, when there are advantages to being small and agile.

2. Which functions should be performed in-house and which should be outsourced? Companies should outsource when they can purchase high-quality services and products more inexpensively or reliably than they can generate them internally.

3. Which functions should be hierarchically controlled, and which should be integrated and controlled laterally? In some areas, organizations should function in a lateral manner, integrating and creating synergies across various parts of the organization, creating cross-functional units to carry out entire processes, and collaborating with suppliers and customers. Organizations also should search for ways to leverage across business units while setting up organizational and management approaches that give the optimal levels of flexibility and control to various business units.

4. Which processes should be IT-based? Today, most organizations are wired and have ERP systems that can do a great deal of the administrative work of HR, but when is it advantageous to have them do it?

Traditionally, HR has been organized in a hierarchical manner (as have many other staff groups such as IT), and it has seen its mission as designing, administering, and enforcing adherence to HR policies and systems. As a result, often HR has been seen as expensive, a necessary evil consuming resources disproportionate to the value that it adds to the company. Among the changes in structure and process that are being advocated for staff functions such as HR are the following:

1. Decentralizing business support to operating units in order to increase responsiveness.

2. Contracting with business units for the services that are to be delivered, and perhaps even requiring services to be self-funding as a way of ensuring that businesses get only the services that they are willing to pay for and that they see as contributing to business performance.

3. Finding the most efficient way to deliver processing and transactional services, such as creating efficient central services or outsourcing.

4. Using information technology to make processes more efficient and to deliver increased value.

5. Participating in cross-unit teams in order to deliver integrated services, to partner with customers to increase line ownership over HR systems, or to bring the HR perspective to various organizational cross-functional team activities.

6. Creating centers of excellence that provide expert services, often in a consulting capacity to the business.

7. Increasing the rotation of people within various staff functions and between staff and line, and having fewer lifelong careers within a narrow staff function, in order to broaden the perspectives of HR staff professionals and increase their awareness of business issues, as well as increasing depth of understanding of HR issues among line management.

8. Fitting the services and structures of the staff functions to the business strategy.

Conclusion

The future of HR functions in organizations is uncertain. On the one hand, if HR doesn't change, it could end up being largely an administrative function that manages an information-technology-based HR system and vendors who do most of the HR administrative work. On the other hand, it could become a driver of organizational effectiveness and business strategy. In many organizations, one of the key determinants of competitive advantage is effective human capital management. More than ever before, the effectiveness of an organization depends on its ability to address issues such as knowledge management, change management, and capability building, which could fall into the domain of the HR function. The unanswered question at this point is whether HR will rise to the occasion and address these issues. Our previous research shows relatively little attention to them in HR, but the growing need for and pressure to change may have created change since our last study.

CHAPTER 2

Research Design

Our study focuses on how human resources organizations are responding to the strategic and organizational initiatives that businesses are undertaking. It examines the extent to which the design and activities of the HR function are *actually* changing by analyzing survey data from 1995, 1998, 2001, 2004, and 2007. We examine the use of practices that are expected to represent the new directions that human resources organizations must take in order to fit with the changes that are occurring in the organizations they serve. We also examine how these changes are related to the strategic role of HR. Finally, we examine the impact of how the HR function is designed and operates on its effectiveness. The study focuses in-depth on nine areas:

1. *HR activities.* To assess how HR has changed, questions were asked about how the activities of HR have changed. Of particular interest is whether HR is doing less administration and more strategic work.

2. *Organization design and HR practices.* A major focus of the study is to learn which organization designs and HR practices are associated with HR being a strategic partner. Of particular concern is whether attention to strategic services, such as organization design and development, is related to the effectiveness of the HR function. We also focus on finding out how much increase or decrease there has been in the emphasis on traditional HR activities such as HR planning, compensation, recruitment, selection, and HR information systems.

3. *Decision science for talent resources.* Numerous books and articles that discuss talent have highlighted the fact that organizations are increasingly competing for human capital and that their ability to successfully compete can be a source of competitive advantage. They also, of course, need to effectively manage the talent. Our study therefore focuses on whether organizations have developed a decision science for their important talent decisions and whether this is related to how effectively they manage it.

4. *The design of the HR function.* We examine whether changes have occurred in the way the HR function is organized in order to increase the value that it delivers. Because of their role in determining the balance between efficiency and customer-focused support, we look at the adoption of shared services and centers of excellence. We also look at the use of self-service and HR generalists.

5. *Outsourcing.* Outsourcing is becoming an increasingly popular way to deliver HR services and gain HR expertise. Potentially it is a

way to deal with changes in the demand for HR services as well as a way to control costs. Thus we focus both on how common different approaches to outsourcing are and how effective they are.

6. *Information technology.* HR information systems (HRISs) have the potential to radically change the way HR services are delivered and managed. Thus the present study examines how companies are using information technology in their HR functions. It also focuses on how effective organizations consider their HRISs to be in influencing employee satisfaction and providing strategic information.

7. *Metrics and analytics.* It is important to know both what measures HR organizations collect and how they analyze them. Thus our study looks at what metrics are being collected and utilized. It also looks at how effectively metrics and analytics are being used.

8. *HR skills.* Critical to the effectiveness of any HR function are the skills of the HR professionals and staff. Thus our study examines how satisfied organizations are with their HR professionals' skills in a variety of areas. It also looks at the importance of the skills needed in order for HR professionals to serve as true business and strategic partners.

9. *HR effectiveness.* The effectiveness of the HR function is a critical issue. Particular emphasis in the present study is placed on the effectiveness of the HR function in doing many of the new activities that are required in order for HR to be a business and strategic partner. These include managing change, contributing to strategy, managing the outsourcing of HR, and operating shared service units.

Perhaps the crucial issue with respect to effectiveness concerns what practices lead to an effective HR organization. Thus our study focuses on which HR structures, approaches, and practices are associated with the effectiveness of HR organizations.

Measures

The 2007 HR survey is a slightly altered version of the previous surveys. It covers twelve areas:

1. General descriptive information about the demographics of the firm and the human resources function.

2. The organizational context that the human resources function serves, including its broad organizational form, management approach, and the amount and kinds of strategic change and organizational initiatives being carried out by the company (expanded in 2007).

3. The changing focus of the human resources function measured in terms of how much time it is spending in different kinds of roles compared with five to seven years ago.

4. The degree of emphasis that a number of human resources activities are receiving and the involvement of HR in business strategy.

5. The human resource function's use of various organizational practices to increase efficiency and business responsiveness and the extent to which human resources is investing in a number of initiatives to support change.

6. The use of outsourcing, the problems that have been encountered in using it, and its effectiveness (altered in 2007).

7. The use of information technology and its effectiveness (new in 1998, expanded in 2001, reduced in 2007).

8. The use of HR metrics and analytics as well as their effectiveness (new in 2004, expanded in 2007).

9. How the effectiveness of HR programs and activities is measured (new in 2004, expanded in 2007).

10. How HR leaders and business leaders make decisions that involve human capital (new in 2004).

11. The skill requirements for employees in the HR function and satisfaction with current skills.

12. The perceived effectiveness of the human resource function and the importance of a variety of HR activities.

The findings will be reported in roughly this order.

Sample

This is the fifth study in a series examining whether there is change in the human resources organizations of large and medium-sized corporations. In the first study in 1995, surveys were mailed to HR executives at the director level or above in 417 large and medium-sized service and industrial firms (Mohrman, Lawler, and McMahan 1996). The executives chosen had broad visibility to the human resource function across the corporation. Responses were received from 130 companies. The second study was done in 1998. Surveys were mailed to similar executives at 663 similar firms, with 199 usable surveys returned (Lawler and Mohrman 2000). In the third survey, done in 2001, 966 surveys were mailed and 150 usable surveys were received (Lawler and Mohrman 2003a). For the 2004 study, surveys were again mailed to HR executives with corporate visibility of the HR function in large and medium-sized companies (Lawler, Boudreau, and Mohrman 2006).

For the 2007 survey, questionnaires were once again mailed to HR executives in medium and large companies. For the first time, data were also gathered by using the Internet. The Institute for Corporate Productivity (i4cp) created a Web-based version of our survey and used it to collect data from 43 companies, giving us a total sample of 106 companies. A complete copy of the 2007 survey with frequencies and means for each item appears as Appendix A.

In 2004, data were collected for the first time from non-HR senior managers. In 2007, data were again collected from non-HR senior managers. Three copies of a manager's survey were mailed along with the HR survey to each HR executive. A cover letter to the HR executive asked that the survey be distributed to individuals who were not in HR, but were in a position to evaluate the function. At least one manager questionnaire was received from forty-one organizations. A complete copy of the 2007 manager survey with frequencies, means, and variances can be found in Appendix B. When multiple responses were received from a company, a mean response for the company was computed and used in all the data analyses.

Staffing of Human Resources Function

In the firms studied, the average number of employees in the human resources function was 410. The ratio of total employees to HR employees was 99 to 1. This ratio is about the same as the ratio found in 2001 and 2004.

The ratio of HR staffing in this study is generally in line with those found in other studies. For example, the 2000–2001 Bureau of National Affairs survey reports a ratio of 100 to 1 (Bureau of National Affairs 2001). Thus, despite the introduction of information technology and the downsizing of corporate staff groups, there is no dramatic decrease in the size of the HR function relative to the rest of the organization. Why this is true is unclear. It may reflect the increased importance of the function or simply that it is a well-institutionalized part of most organizations that is difficult to reduce in size.

Information on staffing of the HR function for the firms responding to the study is in Table 2.1. Of the total human resources staff in these organizations, 46 percent were described as generalists, which is little changed from previous years. Forty percent of the human resources professional or managerial staff were part of a centralized corporate staff function, down slightly from 1995, 1998, and 2001, but little changed from 2004.

Table 2.1. HR generalists and specialists					
	Percentage of Human Resources Employees				
	1995	1998	2001	2004	2007
HR generalist	46	46	43	48	**46**
Corporate staff	44	43	46	38	**40**

The respondents were asked to state the background of their respective current heads of human resources. In 74.5 percent of cases, the top human resources executive came up through the human resources function. In the other 25.5 percent of cases, these executives came from functions including operations, sales and marketing, and legal. This result is similar to findings of the 2001 and 2004 surveys.

Why do some firms continue to place executives in charge of the human resources function who are not "traditional" human resources executives? There are three likely reasons. First, senior executives without an HR background are being put in charge of HR in order to develop them because they are candidates for the CEO job. Second, they are being put in charge of HR in order to make it run more like a business and be more of a business partner. Third, failed line managers are being put into HR because it is a "safe" pre-retirement job. The survey did not ask why this is being done, so we can only speculate that in the majority of cases it is done in order to change the HR function or to develop an executive. In today's business world it is too important a position to use as a "dumping" ground.

Organizational Forms

Most organizations start out as simple structures and offer a small number of products and services that serve a defined market. They have small staff groups and are organized on the basis of functions such as sales and manufacturing. They are often small enough to operate largely through informal coordination. As organizations grow and the number of products, services, and markets increase, informal coordination is no longer adequate. The structure grows in complexity and formality as the organization goes through phases of growth. If the company relies on one major set of technologies and a set of related products that can be developed, marketed, and distributed in similar ways, the company may retain a functional form (Mohrman, Galbraith, Lawler, and associates 1998). When this happens, a centralized human resource function typically provides services to the organization.

If the company grows through increasing its variety of products and services and the diversity of its markets and distribution channels, it may divide into multiple business units, each of which is in itself a complete multifunctional structure. As long as these business units are related, perhaps because they rely on common technology, serve similar customers, or distribute through a common channel, companies usually have a centralized HR function. Here, the HR challenge is to organize the function to allow businesses to pursue their unique needs and strategies while providing economies of scale and a foundation for integration across the businesses where it is desirable.

When a company diversifies to the extent that it houses a number of quite different businesses that have different markets, technologies, and distribution channels, it usually is organized into groups or sectors, each of which houses a number of related businesses. When this occurs, the opportunities for synergy among groups are limited. Nevertheless, the company may continue to add value by carrying out some activities, such as HR, on a corporatewide basis. Alternatively, a company may choose to manage its businesses as a financial portfolio only, and may adopt a holding company form that has little or no corporate staff. In this approach each business unit has its own HR staff.

Table 2.2 shows the breakdown of the 1995, 1998, 2001, 2004, and 2007 samples of companies on the basis of their structure. By far the largest group of companies in all of the studies are those with multiple, related business units. Single integrated businesses and corporations with multiple sectors or groups of businesses constitute the remainder of the sample. The table also shows the number of companies that are considered large in size, that is, having more than twenty thousand employees. Organizational size is important to consider because it often influences how corporate staff groups, such as HR, are structured and operated. Over a third of the companies in the 2007 sample have more than twenty thousand employees. This is somewhat lower than the 47.5 percent in the 2004 study but slightly more than in the 2001 sample.

Each of the three major forms of organization that are represented in our sample face common decisions about how to organize human resources and other support functions. They must decide how much commonality and integration of practice they want across business units, and how much they want to organize in order to achieve economies of scale.

Costs may be reduced by creating corporate HR groups for services that do not require business-specific adaptation. They may also be optimized

Table 2.2. Organizational structure					
	Single Integrated Business	Multiple Related Businesses	Several-Sector Businesses	Multiple Unrelated Businesses	Large Companies[2]
2007 percentages	**23.6**	**43.4**	**30.2**	**2.8**	**37.0**
2004 percentages[1]	22.4	53.1	21.4	1.0	47.5
2001 percentages[1]	25.7	38.5	26.4	5.4	32.0
1998 percentages[1]	23.5	49.6	26.1	0	47.9
1995 percentages[1]	29.1	40.9	26.0	1.6	44.5

[1] Type of structure percentages for year don't add up to 100 because there is a small number of respondents who checked "other."
[2] Based on the number of employees.

by decentralizing or outsourcing the provision of services that need to be tailored to particular operating units. Costs have to be weighed against the objectives of delivering services that are tailored for each part of the organization and that are delivered in a manner which supports flexibility and optimization at the business-unit level. In companies that have multiple businesses, this balance has to be very carefully weighed in designing for optimal HR function contribution.

The Strategic and Organizational Context

Human resource organizations exist in organizational environments that are as turbulent as the competitive environments in which companies find themselves. As companies take measures to survive and prosper, they make changes and introduce initiatives that change the organization, the competencies it has, the way it manages its human resources and its expectations of and relationships to its employees (Lawler 2008). Thus in order to understand the HR function it is important to examine how its characteristics are related to business strategic focuses.

Table 2.3 shows the prevalence of a number of strategic focuses that are often part of a company's business strategy. It also shows that the items measuring strategic focus factor into six types of focus: growth, core business, quality and speed, information, knowledge, and organizational performance. The focuses concerned with knowledge, information, and quality and speed are the most prevalent. Customer focus is the most prevalent single strategic focus. The least prevalent focus is strategies involving changes to the core business.

In 2007 a question on sustainability and one on innovation were added. Both get moderately high ratings. Both of them are focuses that potentially can influence HR practices and policies.

On balance, these data support the point that organizations exist in dynamic environments and have in place a variety of strategic and organizational initiatives to better position themselves to perform successfully. The human resource function, if it is to add value and act as a strategic partner, needs to help ensure that the organizational capabilities and competencies exist to cope with a dynamic environment (Lawler and Worley 2006). To determine how it is coping, we will look not only at how the human resource function is performing and changing but also at how its operation is being driven by companies' strategies.

The management approaches that organizations can take vary widely and should influence what the HR function can and should do. Thus in the 2007 survey we asked the respondents how much their company uses four different management approaches:

- Bureaucratic (hierarchical structure, tight job descriptions, top-down decision making)

- Low-cost operator (low wages, minimum benefits, focus on cost reduction and controls)

- High involvement (flat structure, participative decisions, commitment to employee development and careers)

- Global competitor (complex, interesting work, hire best talent, low commitment to employee development and careers)

Table 2.3. Strategic focuses					
Strategic Focus	**1995**	**1998**	**2001**	**2004**	**2007**
Growth	—	—	—	**3.0**	**3.2**
Building a global presence	3.4	3.2	3.0	2.9	3.1
Acquisitions	2.8	3.5	3.1	2.9	3.2
Expansion into new markets	—	—	—	3.2	3.4
Core Business	—	—	—	**2.2**	**2.3**
Partnering/networking with other companies	2.9	2.8	3.1	2.7	2.8
Reducing the number of businesses you are in	—	1.9	1.9	1.7	1.8
Quality and Speed	**3.7**	**3.5**	**3.7**	**3.6**	**3.6**
Cycle-time reduction	3.5	3.4	3.4	3.3	3.3
Accelerating new product innovation	3.7	3.5	3.7	3.4	3.4
Quality	3.9	3.6	3.9	4.1	4.0[1]
Information-Based Strategies	—	—	—	**3.8**	**3.7**
Customer focus	—	4.4	4.4	4.4	4.4
Process automation/information technology	—	3.9	3.8	3.7	3.5[1]
Technology leadership	—	3.6	3.5	3.4	3.2[1]
Knowledge-Based Strategies	—	—	—	**3.4**	**3.3**
Talent—being an employer of choice	—	—	3.8	3.7	3.6
Knowledge/intellectual capital management	—	2.9	2.9	3.1	3.1
Organizational Performance	—	—	—	**3.1**	**2.9**[2]
Cost leadership	—	—	—	3.3	3.1
Total Quality Management/Six Sigma	3.4	2.8	2.5	2.7	2.5[1]
Employee involvement	3.4	3.5	3.2	3.3	3.2[1]
Sustainability	—	—	—	—	**3.6**
Innovation	—	—	—	—	**3.6**

NOTE: Items with (—) were not asked.

Response scale: 1 = Little or no extent; 2 = Some extent; 3 = Moderate extent; 4 = Great extent; 5 = Very great extent

[1] Significant difference ($p \leq .05$) between 1998 and 2007.

[2] Significant difference ($p \leq .05$) between 2004 and 2007.

Table 2.4. Management approaches						
To what extent do the following approaches describe how your organization is managed?	Little or No Extent	Some Extent	Moderate Extent	Great Extent	Very Great Extent	Mean
Bureaucratic (hierarchical structure, tight job descriptions, top-down decision making)	20.2	24.0	28.8	23.1	3.8	**2.66**
Low-cost operator (low wages, minimum benefits, focus on cost reduction and controls)	38.1	33.3	16.2	8.6	3.8	**2.07**
High involvement (flat structure, participative decisions, commitment to employee development and careers)	8.5	22.6	33.0	28.3	7.5	**3.04**
Global competitor (complex interesting work, hire best talent, low commitment to employee development and careers)	21.2	28.8	31.7	10.6	7.7	**2.55**

These approaches are described in more detail in a recent book by O'Toole and Lawler (2006). Table 2.4 shows that the high-involvement approach is used the most by the companies in our sample, while the low-cost-operator approach is used the least.

Throughout the report, we will relate the way the HR function operates to these four approaches. They are not meant to include all possible management approaches, nor is it expected that any companies will be totally managed in one way. They are included because they provide a useful way to identify the overall management approach that a large corporation is taking and how HR practices are related to the way a company is managed.

CHAPTER 3

Role of Human Resources

A key issue for HR functions is how they divide their time among doing administrative activities, providing services, and doing higher value-added business partner and strategic work. A major criticism of HR functions for decades has been that they are too bogged down in administration and policing, and the results of our previous surveys support this conclusion.

Time Allocation

As with our previous surveys, respondents were asked to estimate the percentage of time that their human resources function currently spends in carrying out five roles and how much time was spent on them five to seven years ago. Table 3.1 shows that the respondents report the function currently spends the most time on service provision. When this is combined with the time they spend on records and auditing or controlling, they report that 55 percent of their time is currently spent on administration and services.

When asked about how HR's time allocation in their firm has changed, HR executives report that there has been significant change in how their function's time is spent when they look back five to seven years. According to them, currently less time (55 percent versus 75 percent) is being spent on record keeping, auditing, and service provision, and more time (26 percent versus 45 percent) on the development of new HR systems and practices and on being a strategic business partner.

Table 3.1. Percentage of time spent on various human resources roles (2007)	Means		
	5 to 7 Years Ago	Current	Difference
Maintaining records Collect, track, and maintain data on employees	26.3	15.8	Significant decrease
Auditing/Controlling Ensure compliance with internal operations, regulations, and legal and union requirements	15.2	11.6	Significant decrease
Human resources service provider Assist with implementation and administration of HR practices	33.0	27.8	Significant decrease
Development of human resources systems and practices Develop new HR systems and practices	13.5	19.2	Significant increase
Strategic business partner Member of the management team; involved with strategic HR planning, organizational design, and strategic change	12.1	25.6	Significant increase

Thus our respondents are reporting a significant movement toward HR becoming a strategic partner and doing higher value-added activities. However, before we conclude that this has actually occurred, it is important to look at the results from 1995, 1998, 2001, and 2004.

The data from 1995, 1998, 2001, and 2004 are almost identical to the data collected in 2007 when the same question was asked (see Tables 3.2, 3.3, 3.4, and 3.5). There is no significant change in the current time responses or in the "five to seven years ago" responses from 1995 to 2007. In other words, there has been no change in any of the responses from 1995 to 2007. This raises serious questions about the validity of the reports by our respondents about how things were five to seven years ago.

Table 3.2. Percentage of time spent on various human resources roles (2004)			
	Means		
Role	**5 to 7 Years Ago**	**Current**	**Difference**
Maintaining records Collect, track, and maintain data on employees	25.9	13.2	Significant decrease
Auditing/Controlling Ensure compliance with internal operations, regulations, and legal and union requirements	14.8	13.3	Significant decrease
Human resources service provider Assist with implementation and administration of HR practices	36.4	32.0	Significant decrease
Development of human resources systems and practices Develop new HR systems and practices	12.6	18.1	Significant increase
Strategic business partner Member of the management team; involved with strategic HR planning, organizational design, and strategic change	9.6	23.5	Significant increase

Table 3.3. Percentage of time spent on various human resources roles (2001)			
	Means		
Role	**5 to 7 Years Ago**	**Current**	**Difference**
Maintaining records Collect, track, and maintain data on employees	26.8	14.9	Significant decrease
Auditing/Controlling Ensure compliance with internal operations, regulations, and legal and union requirements	17.1	11.4	Significant decrease
Human resources service provider Assist with implementation and administration of HR practices	33.1	31.3	No significant change
Development of human resources systems and practices Develop new HR systems and practices	13.9	19.3	Significant increase
Strategic business partner Member of the management team; involved with strategic HR planning, organizational design, and strategic change	9.1	23.2	Significant increase

Table 3.4. Percentage of time spent on various human resources roles (1998)			
	Means		
Role	**5 to 7 Years Ago**	**Current**	**Difference**
Maintaining records Collect, track, and maintain data on employees	25.6	16.1	Significant decrease
Auditing/Controlling Ensure compliance with internal operations, regulations, and legal and union requirements	16.4	11.2	Significant decrease
Human resources service provider Assist with implementation and administration of HR practices	36.4	35.0	No significant change
Development of human resources systems and practices Develop new HR systems and practices	14.2	19.2	Significant increase
Strategic business partner Member of the management team; involved with strategic HR planning, organizational design, and strategic change	9.4	20.3	Significant increase

Table 3.5. Percentage of time spent on various human resources roles (1995)			
	Means		
Role	**5 to 7 Years Ago**	**Current**	**Difference**
Maintaining records Collect, track, and maintain data on employees	22.9	15.4	Significant decrease
Auditing/Controlling Ensure compliance with internal operations, regulations, and legal and union requirements	19.5	12.2	Significant decrease
Human resources service provider Assist with implementation and administration of HR practices	34.3	31.3	Significant decrease
Development of human resources systems and practices Develop new HR systems and practices	14.3	18.6	Significant increase
Strategic business partner Member of the management team; involved with strategic HR planning, organizational design, and strategic change	10.3	21.9	Significant increase

It might be expected that the 2007 estimates of how things were five to seven years earlier would be somewhat in line with how things were said to be in our 1998 study, in our 2004 study, and especially in our 2001 study (six years ago), but they are not. Instead, rather than showing a change in time spent, the 1995, 1998, 2001, and 2004 results are the same as the results for 2007! This finding suggests that the HR executives who responded in 2007, as well as those who responded in 1995, 1998, 2001, and 2004, may have perceived more change in their role than has actually taken place. In short, they may be guilty of wishful thinking and a selective memory.

What should we believe, retrospective reports of the way things were, or data from the past about the way things were at the time the data were collected? The answer is obvious: individuals are much better at reporting how things are now than what they were like years ago. Reports concerning how things were in the past often include changes that reflect favorably on the individual. In this case, it is possible that HR executives want to see themselves as more of a strategic partner now than they were in the past. This is quite likely, given the many books and articles that have called for this to happen and the advantages it offers those in the HR profession.

The complete lack of change in the report of how time is spent is surprising and a source of concern: the results from 1995 are almost identical to those from 2007. It is almost an understatement to say that the world of business has changed dramatically since 1995. Thus it is surprising, indeed shocking, that how HR spends its time has not. It is perhaps less surprising that HR continues to believe it has changed, even though it has not! But this may be a major problem if it leads to HR executives believing they have made progress toward an objective they feel is important when in fact they haven't.

Strategy and Time Allocation

The relationships between the strategic focuses and how HR spends its time are shown in Table 3.6. The correlations in the table show a clear pattern: maintaining records, auditing/controlling, and providing services are either negatively related or not significantly related to all the strategic focuses. A similar result was found in our 2004 study. Apparently, the weaker an organization's strategic focus in these areas, the more the HR function spends its time maintaining records, auditing/controlling, and providing HR services.

As was true in 2004, time spent on strategic business partnering by the HR function is positively related to all the strategic focuses. Although the relationships are not strong, this finding suggests that HR becomes

Table 3.6. Relationship of strategic focuses to HR roles								
	Strategic Focuses							
HR Roles	**Growth**	**Core Business**	**Quality and Speed**	**Information-Based Strategies**	**Knowledge-Based Strategies**	**Organizational Performance**	**Sustainability**	**Innovation**
Maintaining records	.14	−.13	−.17^t	−.17^t	−.28**	−.19^t	−.18^t	−.06
Auditing/Controlling	.06	−.05	.08	−.16	.05	.11	.05	.05
Providing HR services	−.27**	−.11	−.18^t	−.06	−.01	−.12	.08	−.08
Developing HR systems	−.03	−.03	.19^t	.10	.11	.04	−.07	.10
Strategic business partnering	.19^t	.25**	.16	.19^t	.13	.20*	.08	.05
Significance level: $^t p \leq .10$; *$p \leq .05$; **$p \leq .01$; ***$p \leq .001$								

Table 3.7. Relationship of management to HR roles				
	Management Approach			
HR Roles	**Bureaucratic**	**Low-Cost Operator**	**High Involvement**	**Global Competitor**
Maintaining records	.18[t]	.24*	−.26**	−.07
Auditing/Controlling	−.01	.04	−.03	−.02
Providing HR services	.00	−.15	−.05	−.06
Developing HR systems	−.12	−.06	.14	−.03
Strategic business partnering	−.06	.01	.17[t]	.15
Significance level: [t] $p \le .10$; * $p \le .05$; ** $p \le .01$; *** $p \le .001$				

much more involved in strategic business partnering when the organization has a clear strategic focus, regardless of what that focus is. One implication of this finding is that in order for HR to become more strategic, organizations themselves may need to become more strategic. Of course, one way for this to happen is for HR to provide leadership and help the rest of an organization become more strategic. If it can accomplish this, we believe there is a good chance HR will spend more time on strategy.

The management approach organizations take has a low, but in several cases a significant, relationship to how HR spends its time. As is shown in Table 3.7, taking a low-cost-operator approach is associated with spending more time maintaining records, while taking a high-involvement approach is associated with spending less. As might be expected, strategic business partnering is highest in high-involvement and global-competitor organizations. It is somewhat surprising that these relationships are not statistically significant. Particularly in high-involvement organizations, there are many opportunities for HR to play a strategic role (Lawler 2003).

Role with Board

There are a number of issues corporate boards deal with that require HR expertise and information. This raises the obvious question of whether when they face these issues they call on HR for support. Table 3.8 shows the responses to a question that asks about the type of help HR gives to boards. The question was first asked in 2004, so there are only data from 2004 and 2007 in the table.

Two issues, executive compensation and succession, are clearly the ones on which HR is most likely to be asked for help. This finding is not surprising, given that these should be areas in which most HR functions can and should be able to provide help. Nevertheless, it is disappointing that such organizational issues as change consulting and strategic readiness receive such low ratings. On the positive side, it is clear that in most

Table 3.8. Corporate boards							
	2007 Percentages						
How much does your corporation's board call on HR for help with the following?	Little or No Extent	Some Extent	Moderate Extent	Great Extent	Very Great Extent	2004 Mean	2007 Mean
Executive compensation	5.2	5.2	6.2	40.2	43.3	4.2	4.1
Addressing strategic readiness	17.5	15.5	39.2	21.6	6.2	2.8	2.8
Executive succession	10.3	6.2	18.6	23.7	41.2	3.8	3.8
Change consulting	24.0	17.7	34.4	16.7	7.3	2.6	2.7
Developing board effectiveness/ corporate governance	31.6	21.1	24.2	16.8	6.3	2.5	2.5
Risk assessment	24.2	23.2	31.6	13.7	7.4	2.4	2.6
Information about the condition or capability of the workforce	9.3	17.5	25.8	30.9	16.5	3.3	3.3
Board compensation	21.3	11.7	23.4	28.7	14.9	3.4	3.0

companies HR at least has its "foot in the boardroom door." If it performs well in areas such as succession planning, in the future it may well be asked for help in executing change and strategic readiness. So far, though, this doesn't seem to be happening. A comparison between the 2004 and 2007 data reveals no significant change.

The relationship between help provided to the board and strategic focuses is shown in Table 3.9. As might be expected because of the direct relationship to human capital, boards ask for the most help when organizations have knowledge-based strategies. Those organizations that have an organizational performance strategy also have boards that are high users of HR. Somewhat surprisingly, the lowest relationship is with growth.

The use of HR for board compensation help shows only a weak relationship to most of the strategic focuses. This is not surprising, since support with compensation is needed regardless of the strategy. On the other hand, addressing strategic readiness and developing board effectiveness are related to most of the focuses. This result likely reflects the close connection between most strategies and the strategy formulation and implementation process. One without the other is unlikely to be effective. Overall, the more an organization has one of the eight strategy focuses, the more likely they are to use HR.

Table 3.10 shows the relationship between the management approaches and board support. The strongest relationships are with the high-involvement approach. The more this approach to management is utilized, the more active HR is with the board. This finding makes good sense and reinforces the point that when organizations take talent seriously as a source of competitive advantage, HR organizations can and do play a more important role (Lawler 2008).

Table 3.9. Relationship of strategic focuses with corporate boards								
	Strategic Focuses							
How much does your corporation's board call on HR for help with the following?	Growth	Core Business	Quality and Speed	Information-Based Strategies	Knowledge-Based Strategies	Organizational Performance	Sustainability	Innovation
Executive compensation	−.03	.14	.29**	.21*	.28**	.17^t	.06	.21*
Addressing strategic readiness	.04	.19^t	.24*	.30**	.35***	.25*	.23*	.29**
Executive succession	.09	.18^t	.32**	.30**	.32***	.22*	.05	.21*
Change consulting	.04	.25*	.17	.23*	.26**	.32**	.12	.20^t
Developing board effectiveness/corporate governance	.14	.37***	.25*	.25*	.33***	.42***	.24*	.26**
Risk assessment	.08	.24*	.20*	.19^t	.26**	.37***	.19^t	.20^t
Information about the condition or capability of the workforce	−.01	.19^t	.18^t	.14	.34***	.21*	.12	.19^t
Board compensation	.20^t	.24*	.22*	−.04	.19^t	.17	.14	.28**
Significance level: $^t p \leq .10$; *$p \leq .05$; **$p \leq .01$; ***$p \leq .001$								

Table 3.10. Relationship of management with corporate boards				
	Management Approach			
How much does your corporation's board call on HR for help with the following?	Bureaucratic	Low-Cost Operator	High Involvement	Global Competitor
Executive compensation	−.10	−.12	.24*	.06
Addressing strategic readiness	.02	−.10	.23*	.06
Executive succession	.02	−.14	.25*	.07
Change consulting	−.03	.07	.21*	.17^t
Developing board effectiveness/ corporate governance	−.04	−.03	.12	.13
Risk assessment	.04	−.01	.17	.03
Information about the condition or capability of the workforce	.11	−.14	.09	.15
Board compensation	−.03	−.00	.14	.24*
Significance level: $^t p \leq .10$; *$p \leq .05$; **$p \leq .01$; ***$p \leq .001$				

Conclusion

Once again the obvious conclusion is that HR has not changed how it allocates its time. It remains a function that spends the majority of its time on services, controlling, and record keeping. In addition, it has a limited role when it comes to supporting the board. We will return to the role of HR at the end of this book; before doing this, however, we will look at how HR performs its roles.

CHAPTER 4

Business Strategy

The involvement that the HR function has in the strategy development and implementation process—how much and what kind—is a critical determinant of the influence it has and the value it adds. There is a growing consensus among executives and researchers that human capital needs to be given more consideration because it is such an important determinant of what strategies an organization can and should pursue (Lawler 2008). It also may be a key determinant of how a strategy should be pursued.

Type of Involvement

The involvement of the HR function in business strategy can take a variety of forms. Table 4.1 shows that in 2007, virtually all HR functions reported that they were involved in business strategy. However, in almost 70 percent of the companies studied, HR was less than a full partner in the eyes of their HR executives. When the 2007 data are compared to those of 1998, 2001, and 2004, there is no statistically significant change in the extent to which HR reports being involved in business strategy. The 2007 data look like the 1998 data, which found the lowest level of involvement of the previous studies. Thus the data do not suggest that the HR function is becoming more of a strategic partner in most organizations; instead, at best, they show a stagnant situation.

Managers not in the HR function (from here on we will refer to them as "managers") report lower levels of strategic involvement on the part of the HR function than do their counterparts in HR. As can be seen in Table 4.1, in 2007 only 26.8 percent of managers saw HR as a full partner in developing and implementing the business strategy, compared to 32.1

Table 4.1. HR's role in strategy						
	1998	**2001**	**2004**		**2007**	
Role in Strategy			**HR Executives**	**Managers**	**HR Executives**	**Managers**
No role	4.2	3.4	2.0	5.3	**5.7**	**4.9**
Implementation role	16.8	11.6	12.2	18.4	**17.0**	**19.5**
Input role	49.6	43.8	45.9	52.6	**45.3**	**48.8**
Full partner	29.4	41.1	39.8	23.7	**32.1**	**26.8**
Mean	3.0	3.2	3.2	2.9[1]	**3.0**	**3.0**

Response scale: 1 = No role to 4 = Full partner

[1] Significant difference ($p \leq .05$) between HR executives and managers in 2004.

No significant difference ($p \leq .05$) between HR executives and managers in 2007.

percent of HR executives who self-report that they are. This actually is a smaller difference than we found in 2004 (23.7 versus 39.8).

The finding of a difference between HR executives and managers in our 2004 and 2007 surveys is not surprising, in the light of an earlier study that asked HR executives and line managers about the role of HR (Society for Human Resource Management 1998); it too found a significant difference between HR executives and managers in their estimates of the role HR plays in business. Not surprisingly, HR executives saw themselves as more of a business partner than did managers: 79 percent of HR executives said they were business partners, whereas only 53 percent of the line managers shared this view.

The difference in views between HR executives and managers can be explained in a number of ways, among them the fact that HR executives have much more information with respect to their role in strategy than do most managers. Because HR executives have more information, they may have a more accurate image of what their role is in the strategy process.

There is also the possibility that HR executives tend to see themselves playing a more important role than they in fact play. The same type of difference might very well appear with any function that is studied. Marketing and finance executives, for example, may see themselves as playing a greater strategic role than would individuals not in those functions. Thus HR executives may simply be doing what most people do—overestimating their importance. Still, it is important for HR executives to realize that other managers may not share their view of the role the HR function plays in business strategy formulation and implementation.

The role that HR plays in a strategy process does appear to be related to the strategic focus of the organization. As can be seen in Table 4.2, when HR has an important role in strategy, seven of the eight strategic orientations are higher; growth is the exception. When an organization has a

Table 4.2. Strategic focuses and HR's role in strategy								
	Strategic Focuses							
Role In Strategy	Growth	Core Business	Quality and Speed	Information-Based Strategies	Knowledge-Based Strategies	Organizational Performance	Sustainability	Innovation
No role	3.4	1.9	3.5	3.4	2.5[1]	2.9	2.5[1]	3.0
Implementation role	3.1	2.1	3.3	3.5	3.1	2.5[1]	3.5	3.4
Input role	3.2	2.2	3.5	3.6	3.3	2.9	3.7[1]	3.6
Full partner	3.3	2.5	3.8	3.9	3.7[1]	3.1[1]	3.7[1]	3.8

Response scale: 1 = Little or no extent; 2 = Some extent; 3 = Moderate extent; 4 = Great extent; 5 = Very great extent

[1] Significant difference ($p \leq .05$) from one other role in strategy.

strategy that is related to knowledge, it is particularly likely to have HR as a full strategic partner. This result was also found in the 2004 survey. It makes the point that HR is most likely to play a role in strategy when a clear strategy exists and it is related to the organization's human capital.

Table 4.3 shows the relationship between HR's role in strategy and the management approach of an organization. HR is particularly likely to play a full role in strategy when high-involvement management is practiced. On the other hand, it is particularly likely to play no role in a low-cost-operator company. This finding is not surprising; it fits well with how these two approaches think about the role of people. In one, people are front and center, and in the other, they are "something to be dealt with."

Table 4.3. Management approach and HR's role in strategy				
	Management Approach			
Role in Strategy	Bureaucratic	Low-Cost Operator	High Involvement	Global Competitor
No role	2.8	3.7[1]	2.2	2.7
Implementation role	2.7	2.1	2.7	2.3
Input role	2.6	1.9	3.0	2.7
Full partner	2.7	2.1	3.4[2]	2.5

Response scale: 1 = Little or no extent; 2 = Some extent; 3 = Moderate extent; 4 = Great extent; 5 = Very great extent

[1] Significant difference ($p \le .05$) from all the other roles in strategy.

[2] Significant difference ($p \le .05$) from no role in strategy.

Strategy Activities Done by HR

HR can make a number of contributions to the strategy process in a business; some involve implementation, while others involve the development of strategy. Table 4.4 presents the data from a question that identifies the specific activities that HR engages in with respect to business strategy (asked for the first time in 2004). Not surprisingly, according to HR executives, the thing they are most likely to do by a wide margin is to recruit and develop talent. At the other extreme is identifying new business opportunities: apparently, this rarely happens.

After the development of talent, the greatest level of activity concerns the implementation of strategy. HR executives report that they are particularly likely to be involved in designing an organization's structure and in planning for the implementation of strategy. This is a logical area of involvement for HR, and it is hardly surprising that it is rated as a major involvement area for HR. A comparison between the 2004 and the 2007 data for HR executives shows no significant changes in involvement.

This is consistent with the finding reported in Chapter 3 that HR has not changed its time allocation.

Perhaps the best summary of the results for HR executives is that HR is more likely to play a role in the implementation of business strategy than in the development of it or making key decisions concerning what it will be. Finally, it is worth noting that, as was pointed out in Chapter 3, HR is not likely to be involved with the corporate board in discussions of business strategy, nor in identifying new business opportunities.

Table 4.4 also shows how managers rate the involvement of HR in strategy. The results here are consistent with the earlier finding that managers in general tend to see less involvement of HR in strategy than HR executives do. All but one of the items is rated lower in 2004 by managers than by HR executives. However, only two of the differences reach statistical significance. In 2007 the same pattern exists, with six of the differences reaching statistical significance.

Overall, it seems that managers simply don't see HR as involved in business strategy as do HR executives, even when it comes to such specifics as recruiting and developing talent. It is interesting that the relative degree of involvement in different activities as seen by managers and HR executives is very similar. Managers agree with HR executives that the major involvement of HR is in recruiting and developing talent and

Table 4.4. Business strategy activities						
	HR Executives			**Managers**		
Strategic Activities Done by HR	**Mean (2004)**	**Mean (2007)**	**Correlation with HR Role in Strategy (2007)**	**Mean (2004)**	**Mean (2007)**	**Correlation with HR Role in Strategy (2007)**
Help identify or design strategy options	2.9	**3.0**	**.66*****	2.7	**2.6**	**.52*****
Help decide among the best strategy options	3.0	**3.1**	**.67*****	2.9	**2.7[2]**	**.55*****
Help plan the implementation of strategy	3.6	**3.8**	**.38*****	3.4	**3.3[2]**	**.57*****
Help identify new business opportunities	2.0	**2.2**	**.55*****	2.0	**1.7[2]**	**.54*****
Assess the organization's readiness to implement strategies	3.5	**3.5**	**.64*****	3.4	**3.3**	**.45****
Help design the organization structure to implement strategy	3.8	**3.9**	**.63*****	3.5	**3.6**	**.69*****
Assess possible merger, acquisition, or divestiture strategies	2.9	**3.0**	**.53*****	2.3[1]	**2.4[2]**	**.42****
Work with the corporate board on business strategy	2.6	**2.9**	**.54*****	2.5	**2.4[2]**	**.58*****
Recruit and develop talent	4.6	**4.6**	**.27****	4.2[1]	**4.2[2]**	**.59*****

Response scale: 1 = Little or no extent; 2 = Some extent; 3 = Moderate extent; 4 = Great extent; 5 = Very great extent

[1] Significant difference ($p \le .05$) between HR executives and managers in 2004.

[2] Significant difference ($p \le .05$) between HR executives and managers in 2007.

Significance level: [t] $p \le .10$; * $p \le .05$; ** $p \le .01$; *** $p \le .001$

other implementation issues that are involved in strategy. They also agree that HR has little involvement in identifying new business opportunities.

Table 4.4 also shows the relationships between the business strategy activities of HR and HR's role in strategy. Not surprisingly, the relationships are strong, which indicates that these activities are associated with the degree of involvement HR has in the strategy process. The weakest relationship in 2004 for HR executives is with the recruitment and development of talent. However, this is not true in 2007; all the correlations are high in the 2007 data.

As can be seen in Table 4.5, there are numerous, significant relationships between the company strategic focus areas and the role that HR plays in the strategy process. Three of the strategic focuses, quality and speed, information-based strategies, and organizational performance, are associated with HR's active involvement in almost all of the business strategy activities listed in Table 4.5. Knowledge-based strategies are related to five activities. Growth, core business, and sustainability are related to the fewest.

It is a bit surprising that a strategic focus on growth has only weak relationships to the strategy activities of the HR function. It is particularly

Table 4.5. Relationship of business strategy activities to strategic focuses								
	Strategic Focuses							
Strategy Activities Done by HR	Growth	Core Business	Quality and Speed	Information-Based Strategies	Knowledge-Based Strategies	Organizational Performance	Sustainability	Innovation
Help identify or design strategy options	.08	.27**	.26**	.29**	.28**	.30**	.03	.20*
Help decide among the best strategy options	.04	.20^t	.31**	.28**	.27**	.33***	−.08	.23*
Help plan the implementation of strategy	−.01	.09	.28**	.28**	.09	.14	−.15	.19^t
Help identify new business opportunities	.22*	.13	.25*	.24*	.25*	.39***	.02	.35***
Assess the organization's readiness to implement strategies	.13	.16	.27**	.22*	.23*	.26**	.07	.24*
Help design the organization structure to implement strategy	.07	.14	.34***	.31**	.19^t	.28**	−.07	.20*
Assess possible merger, acquisition, or divestiture strategies	.24*	.19^t	.16	.15	.03	.24*	−.01	.10
Work with the corporate board on business strategy	.20*	.23*	.30**	.26*	.22*	.34***	−.07	.27**
Recruit and develop talent	−.08	−.14	.20^t	.21*	.17^t	.07	−.18^t	.17^t
Significance level: $^t p \le .10$; $* p \le .05$; $** p \le .01$; $*** p \le .001$								

surprising that it is not significantly related to recruiting and developing talent, since with growth, talent becomes a particularly critical issue. In our 2004 study it was significantly related. There is not an obvious explanation of why this has changed.

Four of the strategy activities are significantly related to the strength of four or more strategic focuses. In addition, most of the correlations (all but two) are positive. This means that the more corporations have a strategic focus, the more the HR function engages in these strategy activities. This relationship is not surprising, since in order to effectively perform most of the strategy activities studied, HR needs the guidance of a well-articulated strategy. In total, the results on strategic focuses suggest that almost regardless of the strategic focus in an organization, HR can perform relevant and important strategy activities.

The strategy activities shown in Table 4.6 are most likely to be done by HR in organizations that take a high-involvement approach to management. This follows directly from the focus in high-involvement organizations on using talent and organizations as a source of competitive advantage. The relatively strong negative relationship between the low-cost-operator approach and the recruiting and development of talent is interesting. It is consistent with the point that this management approach simply doesn't see talent as a key asset.

Table 4.6. Relationship of business strategy activities to management approach				
	Management Approach			
Strategy Activities Done by HR	Bureaucratic	Low-Cost Operator	High Involvement	Global Competitor
Help identify or design strategy options	−.16	.16	.25*	.18^t
Help decide among the best strategy options	−.06	.11	.22*	.16
Help plan the implementation of strategy	−.04	.10	.11	.15
Help identify new business opportunities	.05	.24*	.05	.23*
Assess the organization's readiness to implement strategies	−.02	.06	.21*	.15
Help design the organization structure to implement strategy	−.06	−.04	.20^t	.12
Assess possible merger, acquisition, or divestiture strategies	.04	.22*	.03	.11
Work with the corporate board on business strategy	−.01	.19^t	.11	.19^t
Recruit and develop talent	.03	−.29**	.15	−.02
Response scale: 1 = Little or no extent; 2 = Some extent; 3 = Moderate extent; 4 = Great extent; 5 = Very great extent Significance level: $^t p \leq .10$; $^* p \leq .05$; $^{**} p \leq .01$; $^{***} p \leq .001$				

HR Strategy

Data on HR's strategy activities are presented in Table 4.7. It contains data both on the current level of HR strategic activity and on future intentions. The results from 2004 and 2007 are essentially identical. With respect to the current level of activity, none of the mean scores are particularly high. The highest is 3.4 on a 5-point scale. It appears that to a moderate extent, HR is partnered with the line in developing a business strategy, drives change management, develops a human capital strategy that is integrated with business strategy, and provides HR data to support change management.

HR is not particularly active in the use of HR data and analytics. Data-based decision making about human capital and data-based talent strategies are the lowest-rated HR activities. A comparison between the 2004 and the 2007 data show no major changes in what HR does (questions were asked only in 2004 and 2007). This finding is consistent with the point that HR is not changing.

The responses for future activity levels indicate that a role in all of the HR strategy activities is in the future plans of HR. In both 2004 and 2007, all of the HR strategy items are rated near the top of the scale (in 2007 all are rated 2.6 or greater on a three-point scale) in terms of the future focus of the HR organization. Apparently, all these activities represent the way that HR plans to be involved in the strategy process. Although this is an encouraging indicator concerning the future of HR, there is still a major question concerning when and if these activities will be put

TABLE 4.7. HR strategy						
	Current			Future		
HR Strategy Activities	Mean (2004)	Mean (2007)	Correlation with HR Role in Strategy (2007)	Mean (2004)	Mean (2007)	Correlation with HR Role in Strategy (2007)
Data-based talent strategy	2.7	2.6	.22*	2.5	2.6	.21*
Partner with line in developing business strategy	3.3	3.1	.70***	2.7	2.7	.30**
A human capital strategy that is integrated with business strategy	3.2	3.3	.59***	2.7	2.9	.38***
Provides analytic support for business decision making	2.9	2.8	.42***	2.5	2.7	.30**
Provides HR data to support change management	3.2	3.0	.46***	2.5	2.7	.12
HR drives change management	3.4	3.2	.56***	2.6	2.7	.19^t
Makes rigorous data-based decisions about human capital management	2.7	2.6	.39***	2.5	2.7	.36***

Current: response scale: 1 = Little or no extent, 2 = Some extent, 3 = Moderate extent, 4 = Great extent, 5 = Very great extent

Future: response scale: 1 = Not in our plans, 2 = Possible focus, 3 = An important future focus

Significance level: ^{t} $p \leq .10$; * $p \leq .05$; ** $p \leq .01$; *** $p \leq .001$

in place. HR executives said they planned to do these things in 2004, but as noted, the comparison between 2004 and 2007 shows no change.

The correlations between the current activity levels and HR's overall role in strategy are also presented in Table 4.7, and they are all high in 2004 with one exception. Data-based talent strategies are not particularly highly correlated with HR's current role in strategy. It is not entirely clear why this relationship is relatively weak, given that they are potentially an important part of the strategy process. One possibility is because effective measurement systems require not just data but sound analytics, good logic, and attention to change management processes (Boudreau and Ramstad 2006). It may be that today's HR data focus primarily on the quality of measures and do not sufficiently reflect the other elements of a complete data-based decision strategy. The correlations for future activity levels are all positive, but not as high as those for current activity levels. This is not surprising since future activities usually are more disconnected from current practices.

What the results in Table 4.7 do show is a clear pattern of the types of HR activities that are related to it having a role in strategy. They identify a useful set of activities that HR organizations should consider adopting in order to play an important role in strategy formulation. However, as already noted, the fact that there is no change in their adoption from 2004 to 2007 raises the question of whether or not they are practices that will actually be put in place.

Table 4.8 shows the relationship between the current HR strategy activities and the strategic focuses of the organization. There are a number of significant relationships, reinforcing the point that if an organization has a clear strategic focus, HR is likely to also be actively engaged in the strategy area. Perhaps the most interesting finding in the table is the pattern of strong correlations between knowledge-based strategies and the HR strategy items. It is clear that when an organization has a knowledge-based strategy, it particularly emphasizes the role of HR processes and measures in its work. This finding is further confirmation of the future importance of HR strategic activities, since more and more organizations are evolving knowledge-based strategies.

One of the other strategic focuses that show high correlations with HR strategy is organizational performance. This finding is confirmation of the relationship between human capital management and most organizational improvement approaches. Apparently organizations recognize that if they want to improve their organizational performance, they need to focus on their HR strategy.

All of the HR strategy items show significant correlations with at least two of the strategic focuses. This finding suggests that all are potentially

Table 4.8. Relationship of current HR strategy to strategic focuses								
	Strategic Focuses							
Current HR Strategy Activities	Growth	Core Business	Quality and Speed	Information-Based Strategies	Knowledge-Based Strategies	Organizational Performance	Sustainability	Innovation
Data-based talent strategy	.07	.14	.23*	.22*	.25*	.29**	.21*	.05
Partner with line in developing business strategy	.03	.13	.24*	.28**	.31**	.21*	.10	.18^t
A human capital strategy that is integrated with business strategy	.04	.20*	.25**	.31***	.34***	.19^t	.23*	.29**
Provides analytic support for business decision making	.04	.14	.21*	.22*	.25**	.23*	.25*	.26**
Provides HR data to support change management	−.05	.21*	.19^t	.27**	.23*	.22*	.26**	.18^t
HR drives change management	.08	.23*	.23*	.19^t	.12	.12	.09	.10
Makes rigorous data-based decisions about human capital management	.02	.21*	.30**	.33***	.27**	.27**	.26**	.25**
Significance level: $^t p \leq .10$; * $p \leq .05$; ** $p \leq .01$; *** $p \leq .001$								

useful activities in most organizations. Making rigorous data-based decisions about human capital management is most broadly related to the business strategic focuses, as it is significantly correlated with all of them but one. Partnering with management in developing business strategy is significantly correlated with four of the eight focuses, while a data-based talent strategy is significantly correlated with five. These results are not surprising, given that partnering with management is a way to be sure that the human capital strategy is aligned with the evolving business strategy.

The HR strategy activities show relatively few significant correlations with the four management approaches (Table 4.9). Although the correlations are low, it is interesting that all the activities are negatively correlated with the low-cost-operator approach. On the other hand, they are all positively correlated with the high-involvement approach. This once again highlights the large difference in how these two management approaches treat talent and the HR function.

Conclusion

Overall, the data suggest that HR still has a considerable way to go when it comes to adding value as a strategic player. In most organizations, HR is still not a full partner in the strategy process. On the encouraging side, HR executives do report being active in a number of areas that are directly tied to the strategic direction of the business. These range all the

Table 4.9. Relationship of current HR strategy to management approach				
	Management Approach			
HR Strategy Activities	**Bureaucratic**	**Low-Cost Operator**	**High Involvement**	**Global Competitor**
Data-based talent strategy	–.01	–.07	.04	.01
Partner with line in developing business strategy	.07	–.16^t	.29**	–.01
A human capital strategy that is integrated with business strategy	.05	–.17^t	.19^t	.03
Provides analytic support for business decision making	.06	–.15	.11	.11
Provides HR data to support change management	–.03	–.18^t	.17^t	–.02
HR drives change management	–.06	–.10	.13	.11
Makes rigorous data-based decisions about human capital management	.01	–.04	.08	.02
Significance level: $^t p \leq .10$; *$p \leq .05$; **$p \leq .01$; ***$p \leq .001$				

way from human capital recruitment and development through organization design and strategy development.

The challenge for HR is to increase the degree to which it is involved in strategy-related activities, so that it can become a full partner in the high-value-added area of business strategy. One finding that suggests this might happen is the high level of strategy activities in knowledge-based strategy organizations. As more and more organizations in developed countries focus on knowledge, it may lead to HR engaging in more strategy activities.

CHAPTER 5

HR Decision Science

The growing recognition that human capital decisions must become more sophisticated and strategically relevant represents a challenge for both HR professionals and managers throughout organizations. Consistent with the tenets of decision science in other fields, the key issues involve not only the overall sophistication and quality of human capital decisions but also the quality of the principles underlying those decisions. High-quality decisions can occur only if HR professionals and other managers understand how human capital affects organizational effectiveness and sustainable success, and if they use that understanding to identify and make key human capital allocation decisions. To date, there has been little research on the decision frameworks used by HR and other business leaders. In this chapter, we present results on the quality of human capital decisions and the relationships between decision quality and the strategic role of HR.

The Quality of Decisions About Talent and Human Capital

Table 5.1 compares the responses of HR executives to those of other managers on questions designed to tap the state of the decision science for human capital management. The first item poses the fundamental question as to whether the organization excels in the most vital talent competitions. Leaders both within and outside of HR rate their organization as moderately effective in competing for key talent. The correlation of this item with HR's role in strategy is not significant among HR executives, but is much higher and significant for managers outside of HR. This suggests that the connection between excellence in the talent competition and HR's role in strategy is more apparent to leaders outside of the HR profession. It may mean that HR leaders see many outcomes of the talent competition no matter what their strategic role is, while leaders outside of HR tend to be aware of stronger talent results when their HR leaders play a strong role in the strategy process.

Managers outside of HR report significantly greater business leader talent decision quality than do HR executives. Table 5.1 shows this is true for the question that taps the definition of talentship: "decisions that depend upon or affect human capital . . . are as rigorous, logical, and strategically relevant as . . . decisions about resources such as money, technology, and customers."

It is also true for business leaders' use of sound principles when making decisions in the five areas of behavioral science (numbered 1 through 5 in Table 5.1). When it comes to the use of sound principles in motivation,

Table 5.1. HR decision making

Decision Making	HR Executives		Managers	
	Mean	Correlation with HR Role in Strategy	Mean	Correlation with HR Role in Strategy
We excel at competing for and with talent where it matters most to our strategic success.	3.2	.17[t]	3.1	.42**
Business leaders' decisions that depend on or affect human capital (layoffs, rewards, etc.) are as rigorous, logical, and strategically relevant as their decisions about resources such as money, technology, and customers.	2.9	.27**	3.3[1]	.48**
Business leaders understand and use sound principles when making decisions about				
1. Motivation	2.7	.30**	3.1[1]	.39*
2. Development and learning	2.8	.27**	3.1	.48**
3. Labor markets	2.7	.18[t]	3.1[1]	.30[t]
4. Culture	2.9	.20*	3.2	.34*
5. Organization design	2.8	.31**	3.2[1]	.62***
6. Business strategy	3.6	.22*	3.8	.19
7. Finance	4.0	.19[t]	4.1	−.03
8. Marketing	3.5	.23*	3.3	.25
9. Technology	3.3	.23*	3.4	.23
HR leaders identify unique strategy insights by connecting human capital issues to business strategy.	3.1	.52***	3.0	.48**
HR leaders have a good understanding about where and why human capital makes the biggest difference in their business.	3.2	.53***	3.5	.54***
Business leaders have a good understanding about where and why human capital makes the biggest difference in their business.	3.2	.32***	3.5	.58***
HR systems educate business leaders about their talent decisions.	2.5	.28**	2.7	.65***
HR adds value by ensuring compliance with rules, laws, and guidelines.	3.5	−.03	3.9[1]	.24
HR adds value by delivering high-quality professional practices and services.	3.6	.32***	3.7	.49***
HR adds value by improving talent decisions inside and outside the HR function.	3.6	.56***	3.5	.54***

Response scale: 1 = Little or no extent; 2 = Some extent; 3 = Moderate extent; 4 = Great extent; 5 = Very great extent

[1] Significant difference ($p \leq .05$) between HR executives and managers in 2007

Significance level: [t] $p \leq .10$; * $p \leq .05$; ** $p \leq .01$; *** $p \leq .001$

labor markets, and organization design, managers outside of HR rate business leaders significantly higher than do HR executives, though the differences are not large in an absolute sense. Notably, all the ratings are at the moderate level or slightly below, suggesting only moderate decision quality where human capital is involved.

Items 6 through 9 provide a useful comparison to talent decisions because they describe decision areas that are more traditionally the domain of business leaders. Here, the average ratings by both HR executives and managers are considerably higher than they are for the talent-related decisions, suggesting that business leaders are regarded as less adept at the decision science of talent than they are in more traditional business arenas.

Both HR executives and managers perceive HR leaders as providing unique strategic insights to a moderate extent. The two items in Table 5.1 that refer to talent segmentation, that is, understanding where and why human capital makes the biggest difference in their business, receive moderate ratings from both HR leaders and managers (Boudreau and Ramstad 2005c).

The question concerning educating business leaders is fundamental. If business leaders are to learn to make sound talent decisions, then the HR systems they use should educate them about the quality of those decisions, in the same way that management systems in finance, marketing, and operations management provide clear feedback regarding managers' decision quality (Boudreau and Ramstad 2007). The results show that this question produced the lowest ratings by both HR executives and managers of any of the decision science questions. It appears that one reason talent decisions are only of moderate quality is that HR systems have not yet evolved to effectively help leaders improve these decisions.

Finally, the last three items in Table 5.1 ask about how HR adds value. Boudreau and Ramstad (2007) suggest that mature professions evolve to a balance of adding value through compliance, services, and decision support. Table 5.1 shows that both HR executives and managers believe that HR adds value to a moderate or great extent in all three areas. Managers rate compliance value the highest. The overall level of value added by HR leaves room for improvement in all three areas.

Overall, high-quality decisions and sound decision principles are perceived as moderately likely to exist. Across all the items, managers generally perceive them to exist to a greater extent than do HR executives, particularly when they are rating their own capabilities. Either HR executives underestimate the sophistication of their counterparts, or managers overestimate their sophistication. While we cannot resolve this question, our experience suggests that it is a bit of both.

On the one hand, managers have undoubtedly increased their awareness of the importance of human capital, and of their role in nurturing and deploying it. HR data and scorecards are more available, providing a basis for improved decisions (see Chapter 11). On the other hand, there is a great deal that managers still do not know about talent segmentation, motivation, culture, and learning. HR executives likely can see this gap, and it is reflected in their ratings. HR executives often say "our business leaders don't know what they don't know" when it comes to sound principles of human capital decisions. It is easy for managers to regard their performance as sufficient, while HR executives more familiar with human resource management readily see that much more could be accomplished.

HR leaders, who see room for improvement that their counterparts may not see, may need to provide tangible examples of more sophisticated human capital decision principles. As with the development of the decision sciences of marketing and finance, we would expect that as the HR decision science develops, it will become clear that competing effectively with and through human capital requires that leaders *both* inside and outside of HR not be satisfied with the traditional HR service-delivery paradigm. They must extend it to include making better decisions about human capital where it matters most to strategic success (Boudreau and Ramstad 1997, 2005a, 2005b, 2005c, 2007).

The results described so far in Table 5.1 are remarkably similar to those from HR executives and managers surveyed in 2004. The average ratings of decision science processes and knowledge do not appear to have advanced significantly in the three years between the surveys.

HR Decision Science Sophistication and HR's Role in Strategy

Table 5.1 shows the correlations between the HR decision science questions and the perception of HR's role in strategy. The correlational results show a similar pattern for HR executives and managers. Both samples have significant and positive correlations between the level of the decision-science items and HR's role in strategy. In organizations where decision-science principles are rated highly, so is HR's role in strategy. The only exceptions are with regard to excellence in the talent competition, where the HR executive correlation is not significant, and regarding HR adding value through compliance, where neither correlation is significant. The latter may reflect the fact that an acceptable level of compliance is simply expected, and thus additional value there does not associate with a stronger strategic role.

It is also notable that for the items reflecting business leaders' use of sound principles in traditional non-HR management arenas (items 6 through 9 in Table 5.1), the correlations with HR's strategic role are non-significant for leaders outside of HR, suggesting that HR's role in strategy is not a function merely of general business leader sophistication, but associates instead with business leader sophistication in areas specifically talent-related.

Compared to similar items in 2004, the correlation pattern of Table 5.1 is quite different. In 2004, the correlations differed markedly between HR executives and managers. The HR executives' pattern was similar to the one shown here, in that most of the decision-science elements were strongly and positively related to HR managers' perceptions of their involvement in business strategy. For managers, most items reflecting business leaders' talent decision-science capability *did not* correlate significantly with HR's role in strategy. In 2004, managers outside of HR apparently differentiated between HR leaders' and non-HR leaders' capabilities, whereas HR executives associated decision-science quality on the part of *both HR leaders and business leaders* with the level of HR strategy involvement. The present results show a very different pattern for the managers outside of HR. Those managers now associate the talent decision-science capability of business leaders with HR's role in strategy, much like their HR counterparts.

The results are even more striking, in that it appears the associations have weakened for the HR executive sample and strengthened for the manager sample. For the HR executive sample, in 2004 the level of the correlations between the business-leader decision-science items and HR's role in strategy was higher than we see in Table 5.1 for the 2007 study. For example, in the items labeled 1 through 5 (motivation through organization design) for the HR executive sample, Table 5.1 shows correlations ranging from .18 to .31, while the corresponding 2004 correlations ranged from .34 to .50. On the other hand, for the sample of managers, Table 5.1 shows correlations ranging from .30 to .62 for items 1 through 5, while in 2004, those corresponding correlations ranged from .07 to .28.

In view of the general pattern of similarity between the 2004 and 2007 results, such a significant difference is notable. It appears that managers outside of HR may be developing a stronger appreciation of the relationship between their own sophistication and capability when it comes to HR decision science principles and the strength of HR's role in strategy. Unlike the 2004 results, it appears that in the present survey, managers outside of HR may actually perceive this relationship more strongly than their HR counterparts, though both clearly see it. This is a promising result, because it suggests that managers may be starting to see that a strong strategic role for HR enhances their sophistication when it comes to decisions about HR and talent, and/or that when their sophistication is higher it is possible for HR to play a stronger strategic role.

We do not know the causal direction of the relationships with strategy involvement. These results might suggest that when organizations achieve high HR strategy involvement, HR executives and managers perceive themselves and their business leaders as better on all elements of the HR decision science. Further, they perceive HR leaders to be better at talent segmentation and providing unique strategic insights.

Alternatively the causal direction may go from strategic role to decision-science sophistication. This interpretation is consistent with the typical situation that we see in organizations, where only a handful of HR leaders are highly skilled at talent segmentation and strategic insights, and many of them developed this ability through fortuitous career opportunities to observe and participate in business strategy. This interpretation would support efforts to get HR leaders more involved in strategy, as a way to enhance the HR decision science.

The causal direction may also be that enhancing the decision-science capability of managers outside of HR will enhance HR strategic involvement. Our results suggest that some HR leaders are already "at the table" and have opportunities for full partnership in strategy development and implementation, but that both HR executives and other managers are not satisfied with HR's capability (average ratings in Table 5.1 are only at the moderate point on the scale). Improving the decision-science capability of managers may make them more capable of effectively working with strategically involved HR leaders.

Strategic Focuses

Table 5.2 shows the relationship between the extent to which organizations are pursuing different strategic focuses and the extent to which they perceive the different elements of a sophisticated HR decision science. Clearly, the pattern of significant associations varies greatly with different strategic focuses.

Excellence in competing for talent is strongly correlated with knowledge-based strategies, but uncorrelated with all other strategies. This is somewhat surprising, considering the high profile that the "war for talent" has achieved. It may reflect the fact that pursuing knowledge-based strategies creates a stronger line-of-sight between talent competitiveness and results.

The extent to which HR decisions by business leaders are made with the same rigor as decisions about other key resources is strongly related to an emphasis on all strategies, except growth and innovation. This is somewhat different from the 2004 results, where most strategies did not show a strong correlation with this item, but the growth strategy was strongly correlated. The broader array of significant correlations suggests that there may be a wider appreciation of the importance of talent decision sophistication among business leaders now than there was in 2004. This is reinforced by the results suggesting that managers associate their talent sophistication with HR's strategic role, more than in 2004.

The lack of correlation between the HR decision-making items and pursuit of growth and innovation strategies is similar for all the talent

Table 5.2. Relationship of HR decision making to strategic focuses

Decision Making	Strategic Focuses							
	Growth	Core Business	Quality and Speed	Information-Based Strategies	Knowledge-Based Strategies	Organizational Performance	Sustainability	Innovation
We excel at competing for and with talent where it matters most to our strategic success.	.04	.15	.11	.16	.43***	.15	.12	.10
Business leaders' decisions that depend on or affect human capital (layoffs, rewards, etc.) are as rigorous, logical, and strategically relevant as their decisions about resources such as money, technology, and customers.	−.01	.26**	.23*	.21*	.36***	.34***	.28**	.11
Business leaders understand and use sound principles when making decisions about								
1. Motivation	−.02	.22*	.14	.20^t	.35***	.35***	.16	−.01
2. Development and learning	.07	.18^t	.25*	.36***	.53***	.37***	.25*	.18^t
3. Labor markets	.06	.23*	.20^t	.30**	.37***	.43***	.28**	.17
4. Culture	.02	.04	.18^t	.27**	.34***	.25*	.13	.03
5. Organization design	−.03	.16	.25*	.35***	.37***	.26**	.23*	.31**
6. Business strategy	.16	.10	.22*	.22*	.17^t	.18^t	.00	.16
7. Finance	.07	−.11	.19^t	.16	.02	.03	−.03	.09
8. Marketing	.13	.00	.35***	.21*	.21*	.14	.15	.33***
9. Technology	.11	.19^t	.29**	.43***	.31**	.22*	.12	.41***
HR leaders identify unique strategy insights by connecting human capital issues to business strategy.	−.05	.20*	.11	.26**	.27**	.22*	.18^t	.06
HR leaders have a good understanding about where and why human capital makes the biggest difference in their business.	−.04	.18^t	.09	.19^t	.25*	.17	.18^t	.11
Business leaders have a good understanding about where and why human capital makes the biggest difference in their business.	.00	.15	.07	.20*	.35***	.20^t	.26**	.09
HR systems educate business leaders about their talent decisions.	.01	.27**	.17^t	.18^t	.22*	.41***	.30**	.19^t
HR adds value by ensuring compliance with rules, laws, and guidelines.	.01	.06	.03	.15	.06	.31**	.04	−.04
HR adds value by delivering high-quality professional practices and services.	−.02	.01	.10	.00	.19^t	.09	.15	.08
HR adds value by improving talent decisions inside and outside the HR function.	.01	.13	.18^t	.10	.24*	.17^t	.08	.18^t

Significance level: $^t p \leq .10$; $^* p \leq .05$; $^{**} p \leq .01$; $^{***} p \leq .001$

decision items in the table. The lack of a significant correlation for growth and innovation strategies is puzzling, and may reflect the possibility that these strategies are pursued by smaller organizations, where formal systems to improve talent sophistication have not yet developed. The arena of talent may remain the domain of HR, rather than of business leaders.

The five items that focus on the specific areas of business-leader decision-science sophistication, the item relating to HR leaders' unique strategy insights, the item that focuses on business leader understanding of talent segmentation, and the item relating to whether HR systems educate business leaders about their decisions all present a consistent pattern. They are all significantly related to the four strategies of information-based, knowledge-based, organization-performance, and sustainability, and less often correlated with growth, core business, quality and speed, and innovation. It is possible that the first four strategies more often rely on a broad-based integration between human capital and other resources. Thus it may be important that business leaders have a good knowledge of human capital decision principles to pursue these strategies. The latter four strategies may focus more on one specific resource or outcome, or be more amenable to a division of labor whereby the HR function is more responsible for decision quality, and line managers simply rely on HR decisions.

The core business strategy is interesting in that it shows a strong correlation with the overall sophistication of business leaders' talent decisions relative to other resources, and with HR systems that educate business leaders about their decisions. It has relatively few strong correlations with business leaders' understanding and use of specific behavioral principles. This may reflect a pattern in which business leaders are held accountable for their overall decision quality regarding talent and human resources, but are not necessarily expected to demonstrate a more detailed mastery of the underlying principles. It is possible that a core business strategy focuses on areas that are more familiar or have a longer history, allowing leaders to make good talent decisions based on past experience, even if they do not necessarily master the underlying principles.

The results for items reflecting HR leaders' understanding of talent segmentation (where and why human capital makes the biggest difference), as well as the three items reflecting how HR adds value, are largely uncorrelated with the different strategic focuses. One interesting exception involves knowledge strategies, which is correlated with HR executives and business leaders' talent segmentation knowledge.

Management Approaches

Table 5.3 shows the relationship between the HR decision-making items and the four management approaches. In general, the results suggest that the level of HR decision science is much more strongly associated with the high-involvement management approach than with the other three approaches. This is consistent with the idea that in high-involvement approaches, there is a very significant reliance on alignment, commitment, and trust at all levels of the organization, and such an approach demands that business leaders attend to talent and human capital issues. It is not that talent and human capital are unimportant in the other management approaches, but it may be possible in those approaches to rely on a more traditional approach in which HR has the primary responsibility for talent management and HR rather than line leadership is the repository of the decision-making principles.

Not surprisingly, the first item, excellence in the competition for talent where it matters most, correlates strongly with the high-involvement

Table 5.3. Relationship of HR decision making to organization management approaches				
	Organization Management Approaches			
Decision Making	Bureaucratic	Low-Cost Operator	High Involvement	Global Competitor
We excel at competing for and with talent where it matters most to our strategic success.	−.09	−.26*	.35***	.06
Business leaders' decisions that depend on or affect human capital (layoffs, rewards, etc.) are as rigorous, logical, and strategically relevant as their decisions about resources such as money, technology, and customers.	−.16	−.07	.37***	.00
Business leaders understand and use sound principles when making decisions about				
1. Motivation	−.13	−.08	.38***	.12
2. Development and learning	−.01	−.10	.38***	.06
3. Labor markets	−.13	.00	.26*	.12
4. Culture	−.14	−.08	.35***	.02
5. Organization design	−.03	−.12	.33***	−.03
6. Business strategy	.11	−.12	.16	.11
7. Finance	.05	−.07	−.02	.14
8. Marketing	.11	−.10	.03	.06
9. Technology	.05	−.01	.16	−.04
HR leaders identify unique strategy insights by connecting human capital issues to business strategy.	−.03	−.15	.25*	.09
HR leaders have a good understanding about where and why human capital makes the biggest difference in their business.	−.10	−.13	.25*	.09
Business leaders have a good understanding about where and why human capital makes the biggest difference in their business.	−.15	−.12	.32***	.13
HR systems educate business leaders about their talent decisions.	−.05	.08	.14	.00
HR adds value by ensuring compliance with rules, laws, and guidelines.	−.08	.04	−.03	.20*
HR adds value by delivering high-quality professional practices and services.	−.03	−.11	.25*	−.11
HR adds value by improving talent decisions inside and outside the HR function.	.03	−.17^t	.13	.07
Significance level: $^t p \le .10$; $* p \le .05$; $** p \le .01$; $*** p \le .001$				

approach. However, there is a negative correlation between the low-cost-operator approach and excellence in talent competition. This is the only statistically significant negative correlation in the table. Low-cost-operator strategies place a high premium on efficiency and low overhead, which often means very lean budgets for HR investments, particularly those seen as overhead. It also means little focus on talent except when considering labor costs. Thus, for HR executives in such organizations, the consequences of a least-cost approach to talent may mean being a poor competitor for talent, and the HR leaders recognize this.

It is interesting to note that the items reflecting business leader facility with traditional business disciplines (6 to 9) show almost no significant correlations with any management approach, in contrast with the items reflecting facility with talent-related disciplines (1 to 5), which correlate significantly with the high-involvement approach. This suggests that the high-involvement approach makes demands on business leaders for deeper capability in talent decisions overall, and in the specific talent disciplines. If there was simply a general pattern of perceptions that business leaders in high-involvement organizations must be good at everything, we would see the same pattern in the more traditional business disciplines, but we do not. Facility with traditional disciplines seems to be a ticket to the game in all approaches, but talent-related facility seems more significant in high-involvement approaches.

It is interesting that for the item regarding whether HR systems educate business leaders on the quality of their decisions, there are no significant correlations. This is not surprising for approaches other than high involvement, which generally showed no association with decision-science items. However, it is somewhat surprising for the high-involvement approach. While the correlation is higher in the high-involvement column, it did not reach significance. This reinforces the finding from Table 5.1, suggesting that even in environments where business-leader facility with talent competition, talent segmentation, and talent-decision principles is emphasized, HR systems have little ability to actually educate leaders regarding decision quality. We believe this places a significant limitation on the evolution of the HR profession and the talent-decision science.

Finally, regarding the items reflecting how HR adds value, the correlations are generally nonsignificant, with a couple of notable exceptions. Global-competitor approaches were correlated with value added through compliance, perhaps reflecting the importance of managing against many varying regional legal and administrative requirements. HR value added by service delivery is correlated with the high-involvement approach, similar to many of the other decision-science items.

Conclusion

HR executives and managers rate human capital decision making as moderately effective. Thus there is significant room for improvement. That said, business leaders rate the development and quality of their HR and talent decision making significantly more positively than do their HR counterparts. We suspect this rating is a combination of HR managers' tendency to be self-critical about their strategic contribution and a very real lack of understanding among non-HR managers of the richness and analytical knowledge that exists concerning labor markets, human capital, organization design, and organizational behavior. As non-HR managers begin to appreciate the emerging decision science of talent management, we suspect their standards of excellence will rise.

A significant new finding in the present survey is that both HR and non-HR leaders associate business leader talent decision sophistication with HR's role in strategy. This was not true in 2004, where the association was only present for HR leaders. It would appear that leaders outside of HR are increasingly recognizing the synergy between HR's strategic role and their own capability to make strong decisions about talent and HR.

The decision-science facility of organizations appears to vary with the strategy they pursue. It is more sophisticated when they pursue information-based, knowledge-based, organization-performance, and sustainability strategies. It is striking that only the high-involvement management approach to management seems to consistently correlate with talent decision sophistication. This suggests that business leader sophistication and HR contribution are higher in strategies where there is a strong line-of-sight between human capital and business outcomes and in high-involvement situations in which non-HR leaders' talent decisions are clearly tied to business and strategic results. High-involvement organizations may create a culture and values that emphasize not just the capability of HR to manage the workforce well, but that it is the responsibility of all leaders to do so.

CHAPTER 6

Design of the HR Organization

The organizational and operational approaches employed by an HR function have a major impact on what it is able to do and how well it can perform. For the purpose of this research, practices and structures were studied that have been suggested as potential facilitators of HR becoming more of a business partner and, in some cases, a strategic partner (Ulrich and Brockbank 2005). The approaches studied were grouped into five scales based on a statistical analysis. The scales and the mean responses to the items are shown in Table 6.1.

Table 6.1. HR organization—current						
	1995	1998	2001	2004	2007	Correlation with HR Role in Strategy 2007
HR Teams	**2.9**	**3.3**	**3.3**	**3.5**	**3.5**[1]	**.38*****
Centers of excellence provide specialized expertise.	2.5	3.1	3.1	3.3	3.4[1]	.30**
HR teams provide service and support the business.	2.9	3.4	3.5	3.8	3.7[1]	.19*
HR systems and policies are developed through joint line/HR task teams.	3.3	3.3	3.2	3.3	3.3	.29**
Decentralization	**3.2**	**3.1**	**3.2**	**3.0**	**2.9**	**.08**
Decentralized HR generalists support business units.	3.6	3.9	4.0	3.9	3.7	.23*
HR practices vary across business units.	2.9	2.6	2.6	2.3	2.5	−.28**
Very small corporate staff—most HR managers and professionals are out in businesses.	2.9	2.8	3.0	2.8	2.6	.17[t]
Resource Efficiency	—	—	—	**3.4**	**3.2**	**.07**
Administrative processing is centralized in shared services units.	3.5	3.4	3.4	3.7	3.5	.11
Low HR/employee ratio.	—	—	—	3.1	3.1	.02
Low cost of HR services.	—	—	—	3.2	3.1	.03
Information Technology	—	—	—	**2.7**	**2.7**	**.28***
Transactional HR work is outsourced.	—	2.3	2.3	2.5	2.4	.24*
Some transactional activities that used to be done by HR are done by employees on a self-service basis.	—	2.3	2.5	2.9	3.0[1]	.22*
HR "advice" is available on-line for managers and employees.	—	—	—	2.5	2.7	.21*
HR Talent Management	—	—	—	**2.4**	**2.3**	**.37*****
People rotate within HR.	2.6	2.8	2.8	2.8	2.7	.31***
People rotate into HR.	1.8	1.8	1.8	1.8	1.7	.28**
People rotate out of HR to other functions.	1.8	1.9	1.9	1.9	1.8	.25*
Hire from the outside for senior HR positions.	—	—	—	2.9	3.2	.07

Response scale: 1 = Little or no extent, 2 = Some extent, 3 = Moderate extent, 4 = Great extent, 5 = Very great extent
[1]Significant difference ($p \le .05$) between 1998 and 2007.
Significance level: [t] $p \le .10$; * $p \le .05$; ** $p \le .01$; *** $p \le .001$

Organization Design

The organization design practices used the most by HR are those concerned with decentralization, teams, and resource efficiency. A comparison of the 1995 and 2007 results shows there has been a significant increase in the use of HR service teams and centers of excellence. Most of this change appears to have occurred between 1995 and 2001—there is little evidence of recent change.

A particularly popular practice from 1995 to 2007 is to have decentralized generalists who support the business units of a company. This configuration is a possible way to position HR as a business partner.

The use of corporate centers of excellence complements the use of decentralized generalists by giving them a source of expert help. Growth in the use of HR service teams is consistent with findings from other studies showing that teams are an increasingly popular way to combine the talents and knowledge of various contributors to deliver integrated services (Mohrman, Cohen, and Mohrman 1995).

There is a relatively low rating of the degree to which HR practices vary across business units. This finding suggests that while there may be dedicated HR generalists supporting businesses, their role is not to tailor HR practices to those businesses, but rather to work with centers of excellence and HR service teams in order to deliver common services to their parts of the organization.

The use of common practices most likely reflects efforts to simplify and to achieve scale leverage in some HR activities, as well as the tendency for companies to be in fewer unrelated businesses. There are economies of scale to be gained when corporations use the same HR practices in all their units. This is particularly true in the case of transactions and the creation of IT-based self-service HR activities.

The relatively strong focus on resource efficiency is not surprising, given the cost challenges that most organizations face. If anything, it is surprising that it has not increased. The most popular approach to controlling costs is shared services units.

The information technology practices show a moderate or lower use rate. However, one change is worth noting. There is an increase in the degree to which HR transactional activities are done on a self-service basis. This most likely is due to the greater availability of HRISs that allow for Web-based self-service.

The HR talent management practices are the least used practices shown in Table 6.1. Employee rotation into and out of HR is used infrequently.

The lack of rotation is potentially a major problem for the HR function because it means that its members are likely to remain a separate group with a unique perspective, and not to be involved in or deeply knowledgeable about the business. There also appears to be relatively little rotation within HR, a practice that creates silo careers and does little to help HR employees develop an understanding of the total HR function.

There are a number of significant relationships between the way that HR is organized and managed and the role it plays in strategy. Of the five areas, resource efficiency is the only one that has no practices related to HR's role in strategy. This is hardly surprising given that most of the efficiency practices are not strategy related.

HR talent development, information technology, and HR service teams are all significantly related to HR's role in strategy. To be a strategic partner, HR needs to use information technology, have good talent, perform its own operations effectively, and have expertise and services that meet the needs of the business. Having decentralized HR generalists is also positively related to HR's role in strategy. This finding provides support for the view that this is a way to make HR more of a strategic partner by putting it close to the business. On the other hand, the negative correlation for having HR practices that vary across business units suggests that this works against HR playing a role in strategy. This most likely is because it typically exists when there is not a strong corporate HR function.

Table 6.2 shows the relationships between the strategic focuses and HR organizational approaches. The use of service teams is significantly associated with most of the strategic focuses, indicating the importance of bringing multiple sources of knowledge to bear on strategy implementation. HR talent development, information technology, and decentralization are also associated with multiple strategic focuses.

Table 6.2. Relationship of strategic focuses to current HR organization								
	Strategic Focuses							
HR Organization—Current	Growth	Core Business	Quality and Speed	Information-Based Strategies	Knowledge-Based Strategies	Organizational Performance	Sustainability	Innovation
HR teams	−.05	.18^t	.26**	.29**	.31***	.22*	.20*	.24*
Decentralization	.36***	.22*	−.01	−.01	.01	.10	−.06	.17^t
Resource efficiency	.15	.13	.02	.08	−.11	−.01	.28**	−.08
Information technology	−.05	.11	.16^t	.29**	.25**	.11	.26**	.21*
HR talent development	.05	.05	.20*	.11	.27**	.11	.26**	.19^t
Significance level: $^t p \leq .10$; $^* p \leq .05$; $^{**} p \leq .01$; $^{***} p \leq .001$								

Table 6.3. Relationship of management approach to current HR organization				
	Management Approach			
HR Organization—Current	**Bureaucratic**	**Low-Cost Operator**	**High Involvement**	**Global Competitor**
HR teams	−.01	−.09	.26**	.01
Decentralization	−.07	.14	.03	.18^t
Resource efficiency	−.06	.16	−.11	−.01
Information technology	−.06	−.08	.15	−.10
HR talent development	.08	−.02	.22*	−.11
Significance level: $^t p \le .10$; $* p \le .05$; $** p \le .01$; $*** p \le .001$				

Four of the strategic focuses are significantly associated with multiple HR organization practices. Knowledge-based and sustainability strategies show relationships to the use of three or more HR organization practices.

There are only a few significant relationships between an organization's management approach and the structure of its HR organization (Table 6.3). Not surprising, the high-involvement approach is related to the development of HR talent and the use of teams.

Future Organization Design

In 2004 and again in 2007, HR executives were asked to indicate how they see the HR function operating in the future. The data in Table 6.4 suggest some important shifts may occur. In both 2004 and 2007, teams and information technology received the highest ratings, indicating that these are viewed as likely and important practices for the future. The highest rating for individual items went to self-service transactional activities, while a second information technology item (online advice) was tied with other items for the next highest rating. It is clear that organizations intend to use information technology to enable employees to serve themselves both when it comes to transactional activities and when it comes to advice.

The results also suggest that organizations will make greater use of centers of excellence, service teams, shared service units, and decentralized generalists to support the business units. At the same time, there is a notably low rating for HR practices that vary across business units, suggesting that companies will continue to look for advantages of scale and common practices.

There is little indication that organizations intend to do a great deal more with respect to rotation into and out of the HR function. Apparently, this idea simply has not caught on, despite the fact that it has the potential to make an important contribution to the development of HR employees. There is more support for moving individuals within HR.

Plans to shift toward the greater use of centers of excellence, teams, and information technology and a greater emphasis on talent development are all associated with HR's having a more strategic role. Future plans in the other two areas of HR organization shown in Table 6.4 are not significantly related to HR's role in strategy. A significant relationship with HR talent rotation probably indicates that when HR is involved in strategy, it recognizes the importance of developing people with a broad understanding of HR. The expected growth in the use of centers of excellence fits with the importance of having corporate expertise that can support the strategy development process. Growth in the use of joint task teams is one way to be sure that in the future HR systems will support the business strategy.

Table 6.4. HR organization—future			
	2004 Mean	2007 Mean	Correlation with HR Role in Strategy 2007
HR Teams	2.5	2.5	.29**
Centers of excellence provide specialized expertise.	2.6	2.5	.28**
HR teams provide service and support the business.	2.6	2.5	.04
HR systems and policies are developed through joint line/HR task teams.	2.4	2.5	.32***
Decentralization	2.1	2.0	.08
Decentralized HR generalists support business units.	2.5	2.4	.07
HR practices vary across business units.	1.7	1.6	−.09
Very small corporate staff—most HR managers and professionals are out in businesses.	2.1	2.0	.16
Resource Efficiency	2.4	2.4	.03
Administrative processing is centralized in shared services units.	2.6	2.4	.08
Low HR/employee ratio.	2.2	2.3	−.00
Low cost of HR services.	2.4	2.4	−.02
Information Technology	2.5	2.5	.19*
Transactional HR work is outsourced.	2.2	2.1	.12
Some transactional activities that used to be done by HR are done by employees on a self-service basis.	2.8	2.7	.24*
HR "advice" is available online for managers and employees.	2.4	2.5	.07
HR Talent Development	2.0	2.1	.05
People rotate within HR.	2.3	2.5	.19*
People rotate into HR.	1.9	2.0	.02
People rotate out of HR to other functions.	1.9	2.0	.05
Senior HR positions are hired from the outside.	1.9	2.0	−.10

Response scale: 1 = Not in our plans; 2 = Possible focus; 3 = An important future focus

Significance level: $^t p \leq .10$; $^* p \leq .05$; $^{**} p \leq .01$; $^{***} p \leq .001$

Table 6.5. Relationship of strategic focuses to future HR organization								
	Strategic Focuses							
HR Organization—Future	Growth	Core Business	Quality and Speed	Information-Based Strategies	Knowledge-Based Strategies	Organizational Performance	Sustainability	Innovation
HR teams	–.17^t	.08	.18^t	.20*	.23*	.21*	.10	.16
Decentralization	.01	.18^t	–.04	.02	–.06	.16	.21*	–.03
Resource efficiency	.08	.07	.06	.17^t	–.12	.06	.06	–.13
Information technology	.01	–.07	.10	.22*	.20*	.10	–.16	.13
HR talent development	–.11	.04	.03	.14	.21*	.10	.00	.01
Significance level: $^t p \le .10$; * $p \le .05$; ** $p \le .01$; *** $p \le .001$								

Table 6.6. Relationship of management approach to future HR organization				
	Management Approach			
HR Organization—Future	Bureaucratic	Low-Cost Operator	High Involvement	Global Competitor
HR teams	.05	–.11	.05	.03
Decentralization	–.07	.04	–.03	.09
Resource efficiency	–.04	.17^t	–.12	–.08
Information technology	–.06	–.06	.10	.06
HR talent development	.08	.08	.06	–.01
Significance level: $^t p \le .10$; * $p \le .05$; ** $p \le .01$; *** $p \le .001$				

Strategic Focuses and Management Approaches

Table 6.5 shows the relationships between the strategic focuses and the future of the HR organization. Most of the relationships are low; however, two are worth noting. As might be expected, information- and knowledge-based strategies are related to the future use of HR talent development and HR teams. These are two HR practices that can lead to an organization improving its information flow and knowledge.

Table 6.6 shows the relationship between an organization's management approach and the design plans of its HR organization. There are no significant relationships.

Conclusion

Overall, the results show relatively little change in the application of various HR organizational approaches from 1995 to 2007. There has been a significant growth in teams and centers of excellence, changes that are related to HR's being more of a strategic partner. There also is a trend toward less utilization of HR practices that vary across business units and a greater emphasis on self-service HR practices. But we did not see greater adoption of such things as the career movement of individuals into and out of HR or joint line and HR task teams.

There are a number of important relationships between the design of the HR organization and HR's role in strategy. These relationships are particularly important because they suggest what HR needs to do to become more of a strategic partner: namely, use information technology, establish centers of excellence, use joint task forces, and develop HR talent.

Looking to the future, as they did in 2004, HR organizations plan to change toward using more teams, using information technology, and improving their efficiency. These changes are most likely to occur in organizations where HR is already a strategic partner.

The results do suggest that an organization's strategy has significant and important effects on the HR organization. The HR organization's design is significantly associated with strategies that focus on knowledge management and sustainability. However, the degree to which organizations pursue other strategies is less systematically related to the use of HR organization design features. This finding may reflect the fact that it is less apparent what HR organization design features contribute to those strategies in general, or that a variety of HR organization approaches may work equally well.

CHAPTER 7

*Human Resources
Activities*

To get an in-depth look at the changes that are occurring in the role of HR, we asked whether the focus on a number of human resources activities has increased, stayed the same, or decreased over the past five to seven years. Our expectation was that there would be a change in the focus on a number of HR activities, particularly those related to HR being a strategic partner.

HR Activity Levels

Data analyses showed five clusters of human resources activities, with two activity items (HRISs and unions) that did not cluster with any others. Table 7.1 shows these activities and how HR executives responded in 1995, 1998, 2001, 2004, and 2007. Just as they have in our previous surveys, in 2007 our respondents reported increasing their focus on all five clusters. The largest increases in level of activity in 2007 are in the areas of organization and planning, and recruitment and selection. As was true in 1995, 1998, 2001, and 2004, HR executives report not increasing their organization's focus on just one activity: union relations. It is hard to see how they can continuously increase the focus in all these areas. Perhaps our respondents are feeling a bit overwhelmed by the multiple demands they face and are reporting that they are facing more demands for performance in all these areas.

A comparison between the 1998 and 2007 data shows two significant increases in the amount of increase reported. Recruitment and selection increased from 1998 to 2007 and increased even more when 1995 is compared to 2007. Not surprisingly, the largest increase is in the recruitment area. This resulting increase undoubtedly was driven by the war for talent that received a great deal of attention during the 1990s. Even though that era is over, there appears to be an increasing focus in companies on the importance of recruitment and selection. This most likely reflects a growing recognition of the importance of human capital in an era when more and more organizations are engaged in knowledge work and see talent as a source of competitive advantage (Boudreau and Ramstad 2007; Lawler 2008).

The other significant increase is in the organization and planning area. The difference is relatively small (3.8 to 4.0), but it is interesting that HR managers are saying that the attention to this is increasing. This may be part of a move toward HR being more of a business partner.

Finally, it is interesting that there is a slight decrease in the focus on information systems. This may reflect the maturity of these systems and the fact that although the focus on them is growing, the growth rate has decreased.

Table 7.1. Change in focus on HR activities						
HR Activities	1995	1998	2001	2004	2007	Correlation with HR Role in Strategy 2007
Organization and Planning	—	**3.8**	**3.9**	**3.9**	**4.0**[1]	**.45*****
Human capital forecasting and planning*	4.1	3.9	4.0	4.1	**4.1**	.32***
Organization development	4.0	3.8	3.9	3.8	**4.0**	.32***
Organization design	—	3.6	3.7	3.6	**3.7**	.31***
Strategic planning	—	3.8	3.8	4.0	**4.1**[1]	.39***
Compensation and Benefits	**3.9**	**3.7**	**3.8**	**4.0**	**3.8**	**−.04**
Compensation	3.9	3.8	3.9	3.9	**3.9**	.06
Benefits	3.9	3.6	3.6	4.0	**3.7**	−.13
Employee Development	—	—	**3.6**	**3.8**	**3.8**	**.17**[t]
Training and education	3.8	3.5	3.7	3.7	**3.7**	.10
Management development	3.9	3.8	3.8	4.0	**3.9**	.18[t]
Performance appraisal	3.8	3.5	3.7	3.9	**3.8**[1]	.08
Career planning	3.3	3.4	3.3	3.3	**3.4**	.18[t]
Competency/talent assessment	—	—	3.7	3.8	**4.0**	.08
Recruitment and Selection	**3.4**	**3.9**	**3.8**	**3.8**	**4.1**[1]	**.14**
Recruitment	3.3	3.9	3.8	3.8	**4.2**[1]	.10
Selection	3.5	3.8	3.7	3.8	**4.0**	.17[t]
Metrics	—	—	—	**3.7**	**3.8**	**.13**
Data mining and analysis	—	—	—	3.6	**3.7**	.13
HR metrics	—	—	—	3.8	**3.9**	.10
HR Information Systems	**4.1**	**4.1**	**4.0**	**4.0**	**3.8**[1]	**−.03**
Union Relations	**3.1**	**2.9**	**2.7**	**3.0**	**2.8**	**−.15**

Response scale: 1 = Greatly decreased; 3 = Stayed the same; 5 = Greatly increased

*"HR planning" prior to 2007

[1]Significant difference ($p \leq .05$) between 1998 and 2007.

Significance level: [1] $p \leq .10$; * $p \leq .05$; ** $p \leq .01$; *** $p \leq .001$

Table 7.1 also shows the correlations between the changes in focus on human resource activities and HR's role in strategy. Not surprisingly, the highest single correlation by a large margin is between change in organization and planning activities and HR's role in strategy. The relationship is strong and very interesting. It suggests that the two very much go together, although it doesn't tell us what the causal direction is. It could be that when HR is involved in strategy formulation, it is because it is involved in organization and planning activities or the reverse.

One possibility is that in some organizations the direction goes one way and in others it goes the reverse. Our guess is that the most prevalent is organization and planning involvement leading to a more active role in strategy development. Regardless of which causal direction exists in a company, if HR wants to be an effective strategic partner, the existence of this correlation makes a strong case for HR developing a high level of competencies in organization design, organization development, forecasting, and strategic planning.

The questions on HR metrics and analytics, which were new in 2004, provide interesting data. Both questions show a relatively high level of increased focus. In 2004, focus on metrics and analytics was significantly correlated with HR's role in strategy. In 2007 the correlations are positive, but not statistically significant. The finding of a positive relationship is not surprising, since metrics and analytics can be key inputs to both the development of strategy and the successful assessment of strategy implementation. They also often provide a signal of rigor to executives outside of HR, one that may result in more HR involvement in strategy and business processes.

Strategic Focuses and Management Approaches

Table 7.2 shows the relationships between HR activities and the eight strategic focuses. There are some important significant relationships here. Strategies that focus on quality and speed relate to an increased focus on design and planning, compensation, employee development, metrics, and HR information systems. This is not surprising, since quality and speed are affected by cross-functional process issues that can be addressed through new designs, skill development, and increased organizational alignment.

The results for knowledge and organizational performance strategies are similar; both are related to employee development activities. The most logical explanation for this relationship is that human capital is a particularly key aspect of an organization's performance capability. To

Table 7.2. Relationship of strategic focuses to HR activities change								
	Strategic Focuses							
HR Activities	Growth	Core Business	Quality and Speed	Information-Based Strategies	Knowledge-Based Strategies	Organizational Performance	Sustainability	Innovation
Organization and planning	−.01	.07	.21*	.28**	.30**	.20*	.01	.14
Compensation and benefits	.05	.07	.20*	.25*	.08	.19^t	.17^t	.24*
Employee development	.16	.11	.24*	.28**	.33***	.25**	.02	.09
Recruitment and selection	−.03	−.03	.13	.18^t	.20*	.09	.12	.20*
Metrics	.00	.11	.32***	.30**	.36***	.31***	.12	.21*
HR information systems	−.05	.04	.22*	.23*	.18^t	.14	−.07	.31***
Union relations	.03	.17^t	.06	.05	−.08	.05	.02	.06
Significance level: $^t p \le .10$; * $p \le .05$; ** $p \le .01$; *** $p \le .001$								

execute either of these strategic focuses, an organization needs to build its human capital. Thus successful efforts that focus on these strategies require increased attention to human capital.

It is somewhat surprising that the growth initiative is not strongly related to an increase in any of the HR activities. Growth, in particular, creates a number of challenges for HR and might be expected to at least be related to recruitment and selection. It is weakly related to employee development, which may reflect the need to develop competencies, particularly management and leadership skills, more quickly in a growing organization. With that exception, a growth strategy and a core-business strategy are similar in that they are not related to HR's role in strategy. Apparently these two business strategies do not entail the kinds of changes that create the need for new HR focuses.

All of the HR activities show some significant relationships to strategy except for union relations, which is not significantly related to any of the strategic focuses. This suggests that any strategy focus is likely to have an impact on most of what HR does, hardly a surprising result, given the important relationship between people and strategy.

An increased focus on metrics shows a significant relationship to knowledge-based strategies and organizational performance. This is not surprising, since HR metrics can be particularly supportive of their strategic focuses, which often affect human capital. Also showing four or more significant relationships are organization and planning and employee development.

There is not a strong relationship between HR activities change and the management approach of companies. The bureaucratic approach does show a negative relationship to organization and planning, and the high-involvement approach shows a positive correlation to employee development. No other correlations in Table 7.3 are significant.

Table 7.3. Relationship of management approaches to HR activities change				
	Management Approach			
HR Activities	Bureaucratic	Low-Cost Operator	High Involvement	Global Competitor
Organization and planning	−.20*	−.16	.13	.14
Compensation and benefits	.04	.09	−.08	−.02
Employee development	−.15	−.00	.21*	.07
Recruitment and selection	.09	−.05	.01	.04
Metrics	.08	−.10	.09	.11
HR information systems	.07	.05	−.03	.11
Union relations	.08	.05	−.16	.08
Significance level: $^t p \le .10$; * $p \le .05$; ** $p \le .01$; *** $p \le .001$				

Conclusion

Not surprisingly, HR executives report increases in the focus of their companies on HR activities. In every survey we have done, HR executives have reported that they are more focused on organization design and development, and the data show that the more they are, the more likely they are to be involved in strategy. Particularly interesting is the increased focus on organization and planning when the strategic focuses of quality and speed, information, knowledge, and organization performance are present. Organization design and development is an area that has not always been a focus of HR. It is, however, an area that is closely tied to organizational performance and business strategy. Providing expertise in this area appears to be a way for HR to become more of a business partner, particularly in information- and knowledge-based business.

CHAPTER 8

HR Analytics and Metrics Uses and Comprehensiveness

Organizations can collect and make use of three major HR measurement types: efficiency, effectiveness, and impact (Boudreau and Ramstad 2007; Cascio and Boudreau 2008). *Efficiency* refers to the resources used by HR programs, such as cost-per-hire. *Effectiveness* refers to the changes produced by HR programs, such as learning from training. *Impact* refers to the business or strategic value created by the program, such as higher sales from better-trained product developers or salespeople.

All can be useful, and, indeed, measuring all three is often required to fully understand how HR investments affect organizational performance. Each calls for somewhat different metrics and analytics. They can complement each other, when they are used together. Cost-benefit analysis has often been referred to as the "holy grail" of HR measurement, and it certainly has drawn the attention of many HR leaders and consultants. It often focuses on efficiency and effectiveness. Understanding the ROI of HR programs is useful, but may tell little about the synergies among HR programs and the value of measures in enhancing decisions about human capital. A combination of efficiency, effectiveness, and impact measures is likely to be the most effective approach, but this combination does not exist in most organizations.

Efficiency measures are basic to the HR function, and they connect readily to the existing accounting system. There is growing attention being given to measuring effectiveness, by focusing on such things as turnover, attitudes, and bench strength. Rarely do organizations consider impact (for example, the relative effect of improving the quality of different talent pools on organizational effectiveness). More important, rarely is HR measurement specifically directed to vital talent "segments," in which decisions are most important. As we observe elsewhere in this book (for example, Chapter 5), the evolution of HR measurement toward more comprehensive and analytically rigorous approaches based on a science for human capital is very likely a requirement for HR to progress in such areas as strategic partnership and HRISs, as well as measurement and analytics.

Use and Relationship to HR Role in Business Strategy

Table 8.1 shows the pattern of HR's use of metrics and analytics across the sample. The results suggest that measurement and analytics remain relatively rare HR practices. The only measurement element used by more than 50 percent of the organizations is measuring the financial efficiency of HR operations, and even that exists in only 50.5 percent of the organizations. The HR measures that are used most (over 39 percent of organizations reporting "yes, have now") relate to measuring the efficiency of HR operations. This includes creating traditional HR data benchmarks, which we include under efficiency because the vast majority of such benchmarks reflect costs and activity levels.

Measures of effectiveness and impact are rarer than efficiency measures. Almost 40 percent of organizations use HR scorecards or dashboards, which we include in effectiveness because the majority of such systems attempt to reflect the outcomes of HR programs, including turnover, performance, engagement, and so on, though in many cases they reflect mostly efficiency measures. The other effectiveness measures are used by less than 20 percent of organizations.

Perhaps predictably, measures of impact are even rarer. Though about 20 percent of organizations report having measures of the business impact of HR programs and processes, only 12.1 percent have measures

Table 8.1. HR metrics and analytics use						
	Uses (Percentages)					
Measures	Not Currently Being Considered	Planning For	Being Built	Yes, Have Now	Mean	Correlation with HR Role in Strategy
Efficiency						
Measure the financial efficiency of HR operations (e.g., cost-per-hire, time-to-fill, training costs)?	12.1	19.2	18.2	50.5	3.1	.34***
Collect metrics that measure the cost of providing HR programs and processes?	8.2	26.5	25.5	39.8	3.0	.31**
Benchmark analytics and measures against data from outside organizations (e.g., Saratoga, Mercer, Hewitt)?	14.1	23.2	14.1	48.5	3.0	.02
Effectiveness						
Use HR dashboards or scorecards?	10.2	27.6	24.5	37.8	2.9	.18^t
Measure the specific effects of HR programs (such as learning from training, motivation from rewards, validity of tests, etc.)?	23.2	36.4	21.2	19.2	2.4	.33***
Have the capability to conduct cost-benefit analyses (also called utility analyses) of HR programs?	22.4	39.8	19.4	18.4	2.3	.12
Impact						
Measure the business impact of HR programs and processes?	11.2	36.7	31.6	20.4	2.6	.29**
Measure the quality of the talent decisions made by non-HR leaders?	40.4	35.4	14.1	10.1	1.9	.22*
Measure the business impact of high versus low performance in jobs?	38.4	37.4	12.1	12.1	2.0	.30**

Response scale reversed from survey order: 1 = Yes, have now; 2 = Being built; 3 = Planning for; 4 = Not currently being considered

Significance level: $^t p \le .10$; $* p \le .05$; $** p \le .01$; $*** p \le .001$

of the business impact of performance differences in jobs, and only 10.1 percent actually measure the quality of talent decisions made by non-HR leaders. The latter finding reinforces our results in Chapter 5, which showed that while HR and business leaders believe they are moderately good at talent decisions, HR systems generally do not educate leaders about their decision quality. Indeed, even the 20.4 percent measuring "business impact" may be an overestimate. Our experience suggests that when HR leaders are asked if they measure "business impact," they often interpret it to mean the effects of specific programs on workforce changes such as skills, competencies, and attitudes, which is effectiveness, rather than the effects of such programs on business outcomes such as financial targets and competitive sustainability.

The findings in Table 8.1 are similar to those found in our 2004 survey (Lawler, Levenson, and Boudreau 2004; Lawler, Boudreau, and Mohrman 2006) and by Conference Board research (Gates 2008). Indeed, as with other findings, the similarity between the 2007 survey reported here and the 2004 survey results is striking. Most of the mean values shown in Table 8.1 are within .5 scale points of the 2004 results. Thus even though in 2004 many organizations reported that measures were "being built," the use of these measures has not changed dramatically since then.

The relationship between the use of HR metrics and HR's role in strategy is also shown in the right-hand column of Table 8.1. Most of the measurement items are significantly positively correlated with greater HR involvement in strategy. The nonsignificant associations are with measurement elements including the use of benchmarks, cost-benefit analysis, and dashboards and scorecards. These weak relationships for benchmarks and scorecards may reflect that they have become so ubiquitous that they no longer alter HR's strategic involvement. Cost-benefit analysis is not widely used, and does not relate to HR's strategic role.

It may be that measurement approaches that are complex or focused more on comparing one organization's HR programs to another are simply too far removed from the language that leaders outside of HR use to understand strategic impact. Benchmarking can help HR understand where HR activities are so inefficient as to be clearly noncompetitive, or where common practice suggests improvements to come up to the level of others. However, strategic success often depends on unique, protectable, and sustainable advantages, something that cannot be achieved simply through benchmarking.

Measures of financial efficiency and program cost are strongly correlated with HR's strategic role. They focus on efficiency but often draw on familiar information from accounting reports. Measures of specific HR program effects are easy to understand because they associate particular programs with tangible outcomes such as performance ratings, turnover levels, or engagement scores. As a result, their existence probably helps establish HR as business-focused and a credible contributor to business-strategy decisions.

All three of the impact measurement types are significantly related to HR's role in strategy, yet all are infrequently available (less than 20.4 percent "have now"). This is particularly true for measuring the quality of talent decisions and the value of performance differences in jobs (a correlation of .30 with strategic role, but less than 12.1 percent "have now"). While we cannot say definitively that increased use of these measures leads to higher HR strategy involvement, they are associated with HR's strategic role, which suggests that there may be significant opportunities for HR to enhance its strategic involvement through greater use of these measures. Interestingly, such measures are fundamental to the evolution of a more sophisticated decision science, as the historical evolution of marketing and finance has shown (Boudreau and Ramstad 2007). We believe that impact metrics are both a precursor and a result of HR strategic involvement.

At least one measure in each category had statistically significant relationships with HR's involvement in business strategy, which supports the proposition that the most effective measurement systems combine impact, effectiveness, and efficiency. The more common measurement elements (financial efficiency and cost) have high correlations, suggesting that they have credibility with business leaders. They may represent an attractive first step in the measurement journey. HR leaders then can become more strategically effective by using and communicating the value of the less-common HR measures (such as the quality of talent decisions), which are also significantly related to strategic involvement.

Use of Metrics and Analytics Related to Strategic Focus

Table 8.2 shows the relationship between the use of HR measurement systems and the strategic focuses of the organization. The pattern we found suggests that different strategic focuses are associated with very different HR measurement uses. They also provide some insights about the value of distinguishing measures according to impact, effectiveness, and efficiency.

The extent to which organizations pursue strategies of growth, core business, and sustainability is not significantly related to any of the HR measurement categories. Among the other strategic focuses, some interesting variations emerged. The "quality and speed," "information-based," and "organization performance" focuses are related to the widest variety of measures, with significant relationships in all three categories.

	Strategic Focuses							
Measures	Growth	Core Business	Quality and Speed	Information-Based Strategies	Knowledge-Based Strategies	Organizational Performance	Sustainability	Innovation
Efficiency								
Measure the financial efficiency of HR operations (e.g., cost-per-hire, time-to-fill, training costs)?	.06	–.02	.23*	.17	.23*	.16	.09	.25*
Collect metrics that measure the cost of providing HR programs and processes?	.01	.08	.16	.19^t	.16	.21*	.05	.06
Benchmark analytics and measures against data from outside organizations (e.g., Saratoga, Mercer, Hewitt)?	.12	.06	.26*	.04	.25*	.19^t	.16	.27**
Effectiveness								
Use HR dashboards or scorecards?	.00	.07	.24*	.22*	.11	.21*	.04	.10
Measure the specific effects of HR programs (such as learning from training, motivation from rewards, validity of tests, etc.)?	–.03	–.06	.27**	.21*	.12	.16	.15	.26**
Have the capability to conduct cost-benefit analyses (also called utility analyses) of HR programs?	.09	.12	.30**	.20*	.11	.31**	.16	.17^t
Impact								
Measure the business impact of HR programs and processes?	.00	–.06	.13	.21*	.12	.24*	.11	.12
Measure the quality of the talent decisions made by non-HR leaders?	–.04	.00	.08	.03	.28**	.24*	.18^t	.07
Measure the business impact of high versus low performance in jobs?	.12	.09	.21*	.17^t	.25*	.34***	.16	.13

Table 8.2. HR metrics and analytics use and strategic focuses

Significance level: $^t p \leq .10$; $^* p \leq .05$; $^{**} p \leq .01$; $^{***} p \leq .001$

This finding is consistent with the emphasis that the strategic focuses place on measurement and performance information.

The "knowledge-based" strategic focus is significantly correlated with both the rarest of the impact measures (bottom two rows) and two of the most common efficiency measures (efficiency of HR operations and benchmarking). It may be that isolating the effects of individual HR programs (effectiveness) is not as important in such organizations, because human capital is so significantly related to all elements of competitive success. Thus costs of individual programs and intermediate program effects are not as strongly associated with this strategy, but broader financial efficiency is. It is not surprising that knowledge-based strategies are associated with measuring the quality of talent decisions, if this reflects a broader organizational focus on decision quality in general.

Finally, the "innovation" strategic focus is associated only with measures in the effectiveness and efficiency categories. It is possible that when pursuing such strategies, the business impact of HR programs, as well as the quality of talent decisions and variations in performance, are difficult to assess because the goal is constantly changing. This might prompt reliance on measures more focused on costs, activities, and specific program effects.

Use of Metrics and Analytics and Organization Management Approaches

Table 8.3 shows the correlation between the measurement uses and the degree to which organizations pursue different organization management approaches. As with other HR practices, the results for measurement uses show that only the high-involvement approach has many significant correlations. The high-involvement approach shows significant positive correlations with one measurement use in each of the major categories, again suggesting that it is often the case that all three categories are

Table 8.3. HR metrics and analytics use and organization management approaches				
	Organization Management Approaches			
Measures	Bureaucratic	Low-Cost Operator	High Involvement	Global Competitor
Efficiency				
Measure the financial efficiency of HR operations (e.g., cost-per-hire, time-to-fill, training costs)?	–.09	–.16	.25*	.02
Collect metrics that measure the cost of providing HR programs and processes?	–.20[t]	–.06	.17	.05
Benchmark analytics and measures against data from outside organizations (e.g. Saratoga, Mercer, Hewitt)?	.03	–.23*	.11	–.06
Effectiveness				
Use HR dashboards or scorecards?	–.03	.05	.11	–.12
Measure the specific effects of HR programs (such as learning from training, motivation from rewards, validity of tests, etc.)?	–.19[t]	–.06	.25*	.02
Have the capability to conduct cost-benefit analyses (also called utility analyses) of HR programs?	.00	.10	.08	–.14
Impact				
Measure the business impact of HR programs and processes?	–.13	.10	.11	–.01
Measure the quality of the talent decisions made by non-HR leaders?	–.07	–.05	.15	–.02
Measure the business impact of high versus low performance in jobs?	–.18[t]	.04	.23*	.01
Significance level: [t] $p \leq .10$; * $p \leq .05$; ** $p \leq .01$; *** $p \leq .001$				

implemented together, rather than there being an evolution in which efficiency evolves to effectiveness and then to impact.

Interestingly, there is a significant and *negative* correlation between the low-cost-operator approach and the use of benchmarks. Without more data, it is difficult to speculate on why this occurs, but one explanation might be that the low-cost-operator approach emphasizes overhead-cost reduction, which likely means a stringent focus on achieving low levels of HR cost and activity. It is possible that benchmark data actually might reveal that such organizations are far below their competitors in what they spend and how much they do in the HR area, so such data are avoided in the interest of ever-stronger pressure to cut costs or outsource. This interpretation is consistent with the three marginally significant negative correlations in the bureaucratic column of Table 8.3. Again, this may reflect a pattern that these organizations tend to avoid HR measurement, perhaps because they rely more on rules and procedures than on data about expenditures, program effects, and business impact.

HR Metrics and Analytics Comprehensiveness in Different HR Activities

In our 2007 survey, we asked for the first time about the measurement of specific HR programs and activities on efficiency, effectiveness, and impact. Table 8.4 examines what pattern of measuring efficiency, effectiveness, and impact exists for fourteen HR programs. The rows of the table reflect HR practices. The columns reflect whether respondents indicated they measured that program with none of the approaches, or if they checked one or more of efficiency, effectiveness, and/or impact. For example, the 17.9 in the "compensation" row indicates that 17.9 percent of respondents checked only "impact," and the 12.6 in that row indicates that 12.6 percent of respondents checked all three measurement choices.

While the earlier results focused on the overall measurement practices at the level of the HR function, this analysis allows for approaches to vary depending on the type of HR program. It seems plausible that the use of efficiency, effectiveness, and impact measures might vary by HR program type. This could be due to the availability or feasibility of measures for different programs, the historical emphasis on measurement in certain areas, or the common decision models used to evaluate HR interventions of different types.

It is not uncommon for programs to be measured using combinations of approaches, but most HR programs are measured using just one of the approaches. It also appears that the sole use of efficiency measures is somewhat more common than any other choice, which continues to

Table 8.4. HR metrics and analytics									
	Measures (Percentages)								
HR Programs and Activities	None	Efficiency	Effectiveness	Impact	Efficiency and Effectiveness	Efficiency and Impact	Effectiveness and Impact	Efficiency, Effectiveness, and Impact	Correlation of Scale[†] with HR Role in Strategy
Compensation	6.3	24.2	4.2	17.9	8.4	11.6	14.7	12.6	.22*
Benefits	2.1	32.6	9.5	9.5	18.9	8.4	3.2	15.8	.17
Organization development	11.6	6.3	21.1	25.3	1.1	1.1	17.9	15.8	.06
Organization design	17.9	13.7	21.1	25.3	1.1	1.1	10.5	9.5	.19[t]
Training and education	4.2	11.6	22.1	12.6	14.7	1.1	6.3	27.4	.20*
Leader development and succession	11.6	7.4	18.9	17.9	4.2	3.2	21.1	15.8	.25*
HR information systems	10.5	46.3	9.5	7.4	16.8	3.2	0	6.3	.07
Performance management	8.4	13.7	23.2	23.2	7.4	0	15.8	8.4	.08
Recruitment	3.2	29.5	10.5	8.4	15.8	6.3	4.2	22.1	.21*
Selection	13.7	22.1	13.7	12.6	8.4	5.3	12.6	11.6	.22*
Career planning	27.4	13.7	25.3	15.8	3.2	1.1	9.5	4.2	.20[t]
Affirmative action	15.8	26.3	18.9	14.7	10.5	1.1	5.3	7.4	.20[t]
Employee assistance	15.8	41.1	17.9	5.3	14.7	0	0	5.3	.15
Competency/talent assessment	17.9	12.6	23.2	11.6	2.1	0	25.3	7.4	.21*

Efficiency: The resources used by the program, such as cost per hire.

Effectiveness: The changes produced by the program, such as learning from training.

Impact: The business or strategic value produced by the program.

[†] Scale: Number of measures (efficiency, effectiveness, impact) selected for each HR program or activity.

Significance level: [t] $p \le .10$; * $p \le .05$; ** $p \le .01$; *** $p \le .001$

reflect an accounting-based emphasis on HR measurement. That said, there are some interesting variations across the programs.

Looking at the first column, showing "none," it is interesting to observe how many programs had a high frequency of checking none of the approaches. Career planning, organization design, affirmative action, employee assistance, and competency/talent assessment all had more than 15 percent of respondents who chose none of the three approaches. These programs are frequently applied across the entire organization, or at least large proportions of it. They also often encompass effects that are complex combinations of building capabilities, motivation, and skills. Finally, they are often designed and implemented at the corporate level, rather than reflecting decisions by individual business units or individual managers and employees, unlike programs such as training, and so on. Thus the tendency to forego measurement may reflect that complexity makes measurement difficult. It may also reflect that decisions about these programs may be mandated by internal or external authorities, so once the decision has been made there is little demand for measurement.

Several programs show a strong tendency to be measured primarily with efficiency measures, including benefits, HRISs, and employee assistance. These programs tend to be organizationwide programs for which individual business units and leaders make few design decisions. Thus it may be that isolating the effectiveness and impact of such programs is difficult, so organizations focus on efficiency-level outcomes. Compensation also shows a strong tendency toward dominance by efficiency measurement (24.2 percent), but it shows some evidence of impact measurement (17.9 percent). This may be because while a large array of compensation decisions are policy-based and applied across the entire employee population, some elements are more "local" decision-based, in that they are under the control of individual leaders and affect individual employees and groups.

Leader development, organization development, and organization design show a marked tendency to be measured on impact or effectiveness, not efficiency. Competency/talent assessment and performance management also show this pattern. These programs (particularly the first three) often originate with business leaders, rather than with the HR function, and they often have extensive involvement by the top leadership team in the organization. This may frequently not only draw attention to their impact on the business but also make administrative budget issues less salient. The decision to begin such work presumes that it is important enough to justify the budget for in-house and outside consultants, significant leader time commitment, and so on. The design of competency/talent assessment and performance management often requires attention to strategic and business goals to connect the program to those outcomes. In that case, it may be that attention is drawn away from the administrative efficiency of such programs and toward their effects on employees and connection to the business.

Selection and recruitment are both most frequently measured through efficiency, but recruitment is also very frequently measured with a combination of all three approaches. This may reflect the economic conditions when the survey was done in 2007 and most organizations were experiencing strong growth and employment demands. It may also reflect recent attention to recruitment as a more "strategic" activity in light of the prominence of global talent shortages and demographic changes that increasingly demonstrate the need for a strong labor market presence. It is interesting that selection does not show more use of impact measures. Mathematical and statistical tools for calculating the monetary value of improved selection have existed for decades, but evidence suggests these tools are not widely known or used (Cascio and Boudreau 2008).

Training/education shows a strong emphasis on effectiveness measures, and the highest frequency of measurement using all three approaches (27.4 percent). This may reflect the long history of attention to training evaluation and the popular emphasis on training return on investment and measures at several levels, such as reactions, learning, behaviors, and results (Cascio and Boudreau 2008).

Table 8.4 shows the correlations between the comprehensiveness of measurement approaches for the HR programs and HR's role in strategy. Comprehensiveness is defined as the number of approaches used to measure the HR programs. Thus it ranges from zero to 3 for a program. The results suggest that comprehensiveness is significantly related to HR's strategic role for compensation, training and education, leader development, recruitment, selection, and competency/talent assessment. This most likely reflects the importance HR executives and managers place on talent management and its relationship to strategy. Measurement of these programs is an important contributor to HR having a seat at the strategy table, because it demonstrates HR's sophistication and the recognition of its importance.

HR Metrics and Analytics Comprehensiveness and Strategic Focuses

Table 8.5 shows the relationship between HR measurement comprehensiveness and the different strategic focuses. The focuses of growth, core business, quality and speed, and information-based strategies show few statistically significant correlations. Knowledge-based, organizational performance, sustainability, and innovation show more. If one includes marginally significant relationships, the information-based focus also shows a substantial number of correlations.

A knowledge-based strategic emphasis correlates significantly with comprehensiveness across the largest number of HR program areas, while the focus on quality and speed shows the fewest significant correlations. This pattern appears to reflect that some strategic focuses emphasize the connection between human capital and strategic success, such as knowledge-based, and this motivates deep measurement.

It is interesting that both the knowledge-based and sustainability strategic focuses have significant correlations with comprehensive measurement across a similar array of practices, including organization design, HRISs, performance management, and career planning. These are areas that tend to reflect organizationwide and integrative talent decisions,

Table 8.5. HR metrics and analytics and strategic focuses								
	Strategic Focuses							
HR Programs and Activities[†]	Growth	Core Business	Quality and Speed	Information-Based Strategies	Knowledge-Based Strategies	Organizational Performance	Sustainability	Innovation
Compensation	.18[t]	.10	.14	.07	.12	.13	.11	.22*
Benefits	.03	.03	.02	.19[t]	.12	.05	–.05	.04
Organization development	.09	–.05	.05	.09	.11	.07	.17[t]	.11
Organization design	.14	.07	.19[t]	.19[t]	.27**	.25*	.25*	.22*
Training and education	.15	.02	.13	.08	.09	.04	.16	.23*
Leader development and succession	.19[t]	.00	.17	.01	.18[t]	.11	.07	.26*
HR information systems	.04	.05	.02	.20[t]	.25*	.13	.24*	.15
Performance management	.08	.07	.00	.10	.27**	.12	.29**	.05
Recruitment	.10	–.01	.17[t]	.07	.13	.08	.01	.10
Selection	.13	.03	.12	.15	.14	.13	.03	.09
Career planning	.14	.21*	.13	.17[t]	.25*	.27**	.24*	.12
Affirmative action	.22*	.25*	.06	.23*	.28**	.32**	.11	.12
Employee assistance	.10	.15	–.05	.15	.20*	.09	–.01	–.01
Competency/talent assessment	.11	.12	.11	.03	.17	.24*	.12	–.02

[†] Scale: Number of measures (efficiency, effectiveness, impact) selected for each HR program or activity.

Significance level: [t] $p \leq .10$; * $p \leq .05$; ** $p \leq .01$; *** $p \leq .001$

which suggests that these strategies motivate organizations to amass more complete data to enhance decisions about how programs integrate across subunit boundaries. In contrast, the innovation strategic focus is the only one that correlates significantly with comprehensive measurement of compensation, training, and leader development. This suggests a greater interest in deep understanding about program effects for programs that are closer to decisions which are made by individual leaders and employees.

Overall the strategic focuses are positively correlated with more comprehensive measurement of HR programs. This is consistent with the general point that when organizations have strong strategic focuses they are more likely to have more developed HR programs and practices.

HR Metrics and Analytics Comprehensiveness and Management Approaches

Table 8.6 shows the relationship between the measurement comprehensiveness of HR program areas and the use of management approaches. As in other chapters, the strongest positive correlations lie with the high-involvement management approach. It shows significant and positive correlations with measurement comprehensiveness in all but four of the program areas. The highest correlations are with compensation, organization development, and career planning. As noted before, a high-involvement approach rests upon deep and comprehensive approaches to talent; thus it is not surprising that it is accompanied by comprehensive measurement. What is striking is how little association there is with the other management approaches.

There are some interesting results with regard to the global-competitor approach. Positive correlations exist with comprehensive measurement in the areas of recruitment, selection, affirmative action, and employee assistance. This may reflect the fact that as organizations pursue global-competitor approaches that require integrating talent issues across regions and national boundaries, the challenges of external talent sourcing through recruitment and selection become even more significant, prompting a desire to better understand efficiency, effectiveness, and impact. With regard to affirmative action and employee assistance, it seems plausible that diversity (of which affirmative action is one component) may become more vital and thus more important to measure when working across global boundaries on a large scale. Employee

Table 8.6. HR metrics and analytics and organization management approaches				
	Organization Management Approaches			
HR Programs and Activities[†]	Bureaucratic	Low-Cost Operator	High Involvement	Global Competitor
Compensation	−.08	.01	.37***	.16
Benefits	−.05	.13	.17	.04
Organization development	−.17	.05	.31**	.08
Organization design	−.05	.05	.25*	.12
Training and education	−.04	.02	.24*	.06
Leader development and succession	.00	.01	.23*	.02
HR information systems	−.01	.11	.13	.12
Performance management	−.11	.11	.15	.16
Recruitment	−.17	.02	.20[t]	.23*
Selection	−.14	.09	.19[t]	.29**
Career planning	−.16	.11	.30**	.11
Affirmative action	−.06	.16	.22*	.25*
Employee assistance	−.19[t]	.17	.23*	.25*
Competency/talent assessment	−.12	.03	.16	.17

[†] Scale: Number of measures (efficiency, effectiveness, impact) selected for each HR program or activity.
Significance level: [t] $p \le .10$; * $p \le .05$; ** $p \le .01$; *** $p \le .001$

assistance may also become significant, particularly in regions where basic security and other needs must be provided by the employer, prompting a greater desire and need for comprehensive measurement.

The bureaucratic approach presents some intriguing results. Virtually all of the correlations are negative with the bureaucratic approach (though most are only marginally significant), suggesting this approach may be associated with less emphasis on HR, including measurement.

Conclusion

There is significant variability in how much organizations use the different types of HR measures. Efficiency measures are used the most, effectiveness measures next, and impact measures the least. Overall, no measurement tested is used by much over 50 percent of all companies, and some are used by only 10 percent. Clearly there is room for HR to do more measurement, and there is reason to believe that it would have a positive impact.

The use of HR measures and analytics is significantly related to HR's role in strategy. It is also important to note that all measurement elements are not equal when it comes to strategy. All the impact measures were significantly associated with HR's role in strategy, as was the effectiveness measure of tracking the specific effects of HR programs, and the efficiency measures of financial efficiency and program cost.

Measures that are often thought to be related to HR effectiveness and strategic influence (such as benchmarking, cost-benefit analysis, and scorecards) were found to be unrelated or only marginally related to HR's strategic role. The results for scorecards are in contrast to the 2004 survey, where they were significantly related to HR's strategic role, suggesting perhaps that the bar is rising, with scorecards being seen as a minimum expectation but not a distinction. There appears to be an identifiable pattern of measurement systems that combine efficiency, effectiveness, and impact—particularly evident in organizations with a strategic focus on quality and speed, information, and organizational performance, and in organizations pursuing a high-involvement approach.

The comprehensiveness of measurement is positively related to HR's role in strategy for many but not all HR programs. The comprehensiveness of measurement by HR program varied significantly across strategic focuses, suggesting that it is not just that HR measurement is related to HR's role in strategy, but that the nature of the most strategically valuable measurement may vary with the strategic approach the organization pursues.

Overall, our results present tantalizing evidence that there may be systematic variations in how HR measures are used, and that the pattern of use significantly relates to the strategies and approaches of the organization, as well as HR's strategic role. There is no doubt that HR metrics and analytics are underdeveloped and underutilized. Increasing the attention given to HR metrics and analytics seems to be called for, considering the potential for improvement and added value.

CHAPTER 9

HR Analytics and Metrics Effectiveness

It is very important to examine the effectiveness of the HR measures and analytics used by organizations. This chapter focuses on two effectiveness areas that were studied for the first time in our 2004 survey: strategic contributions (such as assessing and improving human capital strategy and assessing the feasibility of new business strategies) and HR functional and operational strategies (such as improving HR department operations and evaluating HR practices). It also focuses on four effectiveness items we added to the 2007 survey to reflect the LAMP framework, which identifies four vital features of measurement systems for driving strategic change (Boudreau and Ramstad 2006).

The four LAMP elements are

1. Logic (frameworks that articulate the connections between talent and strategic success, as well as the principles and conditions that predict individual and organizational behavior)

2. Analytics (tools and techniques to transform data into rigorous and relevant insights, for example, statistical analysis, research design, and so on)

3. Measures (the numbers and indices calculated from data systems)

4. Process (communication and knowledge transfer mechanisms through which the information becomes accepted and acted upon by key organization decision makers)

HR Metrics and Analytics Effectiveness

Table 9.1 shows the results regarding the effectiveness of HR measurement systems in contributing to outcomes related to strategic contributions, HR functional and operational contributions, and the four LAMP elements. Overall, the picture is one of rather low effectiveness ratings. For no outcomes are HR measures and analytics rated effective or very effective by more than 40 percent of the respondents. Indeed, for only four outcomes are HR measures and analytics rated as effective or very effective by more than 30 percent of respondents. Three of these are outcomes related to strategic contributions: "Supporting organizational change efforts," "Contributing to decisions about business strategy and human capital management," and "Identifying where talent has the greatest potential for strategic impact." One of them is related to the HR function and its operation: "Assessing and improving the HR department operations."

Table 9.1. HR metrics and analytics effectiveness

Outcomes	Percentages					Mean	Correlation with HR Role in Strategy
	Very Ineffective	Ineffective	Somewhat Effective	Effective	Very Effective		
Strategy Contributions							
Supporting organizational change efforts	9.3	15.5	39.2	29.9	6.2	3.1	.28**
Contributing to decisions about business strategy and human capital management	9.4	22.9	36.5	24.0	7.3	3.0	.38***
Assessing and improving the human capital strategy of the company	9.3	25.8	37.1	24.7	3.1	2.9	.33***
Identifying where talent has the greatest potential for strategic impact	11.3	18.6	39.2	25.8	5.2	3.0	.22*
Making decisions and recommendations that reflect your company's competitive situation	13.4	17.5	44.3	20.6	4.1	2.9	.18^t
Connecting human capital practices to organizational performance	20.6	24.7	42.3	11.3	1.0	2.5	.28**
Assessing the feasibility of new business strategies	18.9	23.2	45.3	10.5	2.1	2.5	.33***
HR Functional and Operational Contributions							
Assessing and improving the HR department operations	7.2	24.7	30.9	33.0	4.1	3.0	.26*
Evaluating the effectiveness of most HR programs and practices	10.3	23.7	45.4	17.5	3.1	2.8	.21*
Assessing HR programs before they are implemented—not just after they are operational	12.5	30.2	38.5	14.6	4.2	2.7	.21*
Pinpointing HR programs that should be discontinued	14.4	30.9	40.2	10.3	4.1	2.6	.26**
Logic, Analysis, Measurement, and Process (LAMP)							
Using logical principles that clearly connect talent to organization success	11.5	27.1	35.4	24.0	2.1	2.8	.29**
Using advanced data analysis and statistics	21.6	33.0	28.9	12.4	4.1	2.4	.19^t
Providing high-quality (complete, timely, accessible) talent measurements	16.7	36.5	34.4	8.3	4.2	2.5	.20*
Motivating users to take appropriate action	12.5	34.4	37.5	13.5	2.1	2.6	.27**

Significance level: $^t p \leq .10$; $* p \leq .05$; $** p \leq .01$; $*** p \leq .001$

Overall, the effectiveness of HR measurement and analytics falls very close to the middle choice (somewhat effective) of the 5-point scale, suggesting improvement is possible in all areas. This pattern is similar to our results from the 2004 survey, but there are a few differences. The effectiveness rating on "assessing and improving HR operations" is lower in the 2007 survey than in 2004 (3.0 versus 3.4). In 2004 only the "supporting organizational change" item achieved more than 30 percent rating it effective or very effective, whereas in 2007 three of the items regarding strategic contributions reached this level. Still, the average ratings in 2007 are very similar to those from 2004, suggesting that progress is small or nonexistent.

Regarding the four new items reflecting the LAMP framework (at the bottom of Table 9.1), respondents reported roughly equal levels of effectiveness for all four measurement system elements. This contradicts much of the anecdotal evidence we encounter. Most organizations we work with report that the ability to generate measurements is well-developed, and that they have good data-analysis capabilities. Failure of measures to induce strategic change is usually attributed to a lack of logical frameworks to help those receiving the measures make sense of the information (such as understanding how an engagement score or a turnover rate connects to business success), and/or the failure to convey the information so that it motivates and directs the right decisions and actions. In contrast, the ratings in Table 9.1 are low for all four LAMP areas, leaving significant opportunity for improvement.

Table 9.1 also contains the correlations between the rated effectiveness of HR measures and analytics and HR's role in strategy. All but two of the outcomes show a positive and significant relationship with HR's role in strategy. Even the two that do not, "Making decisions and recommendations that reflect your company's competitive situation" and "Using advanced data analysis and statistics," are nearly significant. Among the highest correlations are the ones for "Contributing to decisions about business strategy and human capital management" and "Assessing and improving the human capital strategy of the company," suggesting that these outcomes either become more common in HR organizations that achieve a strong strategic role, or that they make HR a more effective contributor to that role. Our belief is that both occur because these measurement areas refer specifically to the connections between business and human capital strategy. This type of measure is what HR needs to develop in order to be a strategic partner.

A third item also has a particularly high correlation, "Assessing the feasibility of new business strategies." This item is also highly correlated to HR's strategy role in the 2004 survey, suggesting to us that developing effective HR measures to assess business strategies may be a good way for HR to become more of a strategic partner. Similarly, it is notable that all four elements of the LAMP framework are positively related to HR's role in strategy. This supports the idea that the four elements work together to support or to help advance HR's strategic role (Boudreau and Ramstad 2007; Cascio and Boudreau 2008).

We often encounter HR and business leaders who believe that the HR profession must first "get its own house in order," by improving measurement of, and achieving, its own functional effectiveness, and that only after doing so should it focus on strategic effectiveness. The results reported here suggest that strategy and HR functional measurement effectiveness both contribute to a strong strategic role, supporting the idea of developing measurement systems that are effective at strategic outcomes, even if HR functional and operational outcomes are not yet perfect.

HR Metrics and Analytics Effectiveness and Strategic Focuses

Table 9.2 shows the relationship between the effectiveness of HR measures and analytics and the different strategic focuses. The growth and core business focuses show no significant correlations with any of the measurement effectiveness areas. The quality and speed as well as the innovation focus show a few marginally significant correlations, but are also generally not correlated with most of the effectiveness areas. As before, we think that this may be due to the fact that these strategies often require a very specific focus on one particular outcome, and thus may not require or benefit as much from systemic enhancements of HR effectiveness, in this case the effectiveness of HR measures.

The correlation pattern for knowledge-based and organization-performance strategies shows significant positive correlations with effectiveness in all of the measurement outcomes and the four LAMP dimensions. Clearly, the emphasis on these strategies carries very different implications for HR measurement effectiveness than for the other strategies. Our data are not sufficient to explain this difference, but it is possible that knowledge-based and organization-performance strategies rely more upon a requirement for organizational integration and employee understanding and involvement. Certainly knowledge-based strategies are explicitly built upon an attribute of human capital. It is also possible that organization performance strategies require developing innovative HR ways to enhance overall performance in existing strategic areas.

The sustainability and information-based strategic focuses show some interesting contrasts. The information-based focus correlates strongly with the first three strategic measurement contributions, which focus on HR's role in honing the human capital strategy and organization change efforts. However, it does not correlate strongly with the last four strategic contributions that reflect broader contributions to the strategy process itself, beyond HR and organization change. Perhaps not surprisingly, this strategic focus also correlates positively with the use of advanced data analysis and statistics and assessing HR programs before they are implemented, which is consistent with a culture that emphasizes data and simulations of decisions before they are made.

The sustainability strategic focus shows strong correlations with the last four strategic contributions, suggesting that for this strategy measures

Outcomes	Strategic Focuses							
	Growth	Core Business	Quality and Speed	Information-Based Strategies	Knowledge-Based Strategies	Organizational Performance	Sustainability	Innovation
Strategy Contributions								
Supporting organizational change efforts	.05	.14	.10	.21*	.21*	.27**	.14	.06
Contributing to decisions about business strategy and human capital management	–.02	.09	.14	.27**	.33***	.26**	.20^t	.17^t
Assessing and improving the human capital strategy of the company	–.05	.04	.15	.24*	.40***	.27**	.22*	.17
Identifying where talent has the greatest potential for strategic impact	.03	.09	.14	.05	.32**	.35***	.30**	.13
Making decisions and recommendations that reflect your company's competitive situation	–.01	.03	.06	.06	.31**	.28**	.25*	–.01
Connecting human capital practices to organizational performance	.06	.10	.13	.13	.32***	.35***	.24*	.17
Assessing the feasibility of new business strategies	–.05	.12	.01	.16	.25*	.24*	.23*	–.01
HR Functional and Operational Contributions								
Assessing and improving the HR department operations	.00	–.01	.04	.08	.34***	.21*	.19^t	.15
Evaluating the effectiveness of most HR programs and practices	.03	.02	.09	.07	.22*	.22*	.19^t	.11
Assessing HR programs before they are implemented—not just after they are operational	.07	.14	.08	.21*	.20*	.25*	.12	.17^t
Pinpointing HR programs that should be discontinued	.05	.07	.05	.17^t	.21*	.23*	.11	.04
Logic, Analysis, Measurement, and Process (LAMP)								
Using logical principles that clearly connect talent to organization success	.07	.11	.20^t	.17	.31**	.31**	.16	.19^t
Using advanced data analysis and statistics	.07	.12	.23*	.27**	.26*	.34***	.18^t	.24*
Providing high-quality (complete, timely, accessible) talent measurements	.11	.13	.20^t	.05	.32***	.32***	.22*	.20^t
Motivating users to take appropriate action	.14	.13	.09	.10	.24*	.25*	.18^t	.10

Significance level: $^t p \leq .10$; $^* p \leq .05$; $^{**} p \leq .01$; $^{***} p \leq .001$

Table 9.2. HR metrics and analytics effectiveness and strategic focuses

make the biggest difference when they contribute directly to the strategy process and competitive analysis. The sustainability focus also correlates strongly with providing high-quality and timely measurements. This may reflect the greater emphasis on HR tracking human capital practices and outcomes to show employment practices as a significant element of sustainability and corporate responsibility.

HR Metrics and Analytics Effectiveness and Management Approaches

The results for the four organization management approaches are similar to those we have observed for the other areas. Table 9.3 presents the correlations between these approaches and the effectiveness of HR measures and analytics.

Once again, the high-involvement approach shows strong correlations with HR effectiveness—in this case the effectiveness of HR measures—while the other approaches do not. The high-involvement approach is

Table 9.3. HR metrics and analytics effectiveness and organization management approaches				
	Organization Management Approaches			
Outcomes	Bureaucratic	Low-Cost Operator	High Involvement	Global Competitor
Strategy Contributions				
Supporting organizational change efforts	−.13	−.00	.26**	.07
Contributing to decisions about business strategy and human capital management	−.04	.01	.21*	.04
Assessing and improving the human capital strategy of the company	−.07	−.16	.25*	.05
Identifying where talent has the greatest potential for strategic impact	−.07	−.06	.21*	.08
Making decisions and recommendations that reflect your company's competitive situation	−.08	−.10	.17	.08
Connecting human capital practices to organizational performance	−.13	.02	.16	.06
Assessing the feasibility of new business strategies	−.10	.03	.24*	.07
HR Functional and Operational Contributions				
Assessing and improving the HR department operations	−.09	−.09	.26*	.03
Evaluating the effectiveness of most HR programs and practices	−.09	−.12	.27**	.04
Assessing HR programs before they are implemented—not just after they are operational	−.03	−.06	.14	−.05
Pinpointing HR programs that should be discontinued	−.19^t	.02	.26**	.05
Logic, Analysis, Measurement, and Process (LAMP)				
Using logical principles that clearly connect talent to organization success	−.08	.03	.20*	.10
Using advanced data analysis and statistics	.05	−.04	.11	.03
Providing high-quality (complete, timely, accessible) talent measurements	−.02	.01	.20^t	.07
Motivating users to take appropriate action	.02	.03	.14	.03
Significance level: ^t $p \le .10$; * $p \le .05$; ** $p \le .01$; *** $p \le .001$				

associated with effectiveness in both the strategic and the HR functional-operational areas. It is also associated with the logic element of the LAMP framework, and marginally associated with the measures element, suggesting that getting the logical "story" right and then populating it with measurements may be particularly important. This is consistent with the need in high-involvement organizations to gain strong strategic commitment and understanding throughout the organization, including regarding the logical connections between talent and organizational success.

As Table 9.3 shows, the bureaucratic approach exhibits a consistent pattern of *negative* correlations with the HR measurement and analytics effectiveness outcomes. Only one reaches marginal significance ("Pinpointing HR programs that should be discontinued"), but the pattern is striking. It suggests that the greater the emphasis on this approach the lower the effectiveness of HR measures. Not to make too much of the one marginally significant correlation, but it is interesting that the more bureaucratic the approach, the less HR measures are effective at pinpointing programs to discontinue. Perhaps this reflects the common observation that in bureaucratic organizations it is very difficult to discontinue a "pet" program, or for that matter any program, even if it may have outlived its effectiveness.

Conclusion

The results for the effectiveness of HR measures and analytics in many ways reinforce the findings from Chapter 8 on measure use and strategy. Across a wide array of effectiveness outcomes, there is a consistent pattern of positive correlations with HR's role in strategy. These correlations are slightly lower for effectiveness related to HR functional and operational outcomes than for strategic outcomes, but unlike the results of our 2004 survey, even effectiveness in HR functional and operational areas proved to be related to the strength of HR's strategic role.

Our results show a strong relationship between the four LAMP elements and HR's strategic role, supporting the point that all four elements are necessary for a strategically effective measurement system. Of course, the causal direction cannot be discerned from our data, so it may be that as HR organizations become more strategically involved and relevant, organizations perceive or support more effective HR measures. It seems plausible, however, that at least some of the effect may be through more effective measures leading to greater strategic contribution from HR.

The results for strategic focuses further suggest that organizations pursuing knowledge-based and performance-based strategies are more likely to have measurement effectiveness across a wide array of outcomes than are other strategies, including growth, core-business, and quality and speed. While not definitive, these results suggest that effective HR measurement may be more readily accepted and used in certain strategic situations. It is also possible that broad-based excellence in HR measurement may be less necessary in more focused strategies than in those that rely on broad-based talent understanding or involvement.

In general, the potential for HR measurement and analysis to contribute to HR's strategic value appears significant, while the perceived effectiveness levels remain stubbornly moderate. Leaders both inside and outside of HR may find great value in pursuing HR measurement effectiveness at both a strategic and a functional level, and through a balanced approach of logic, analytics, measures, and process.

CHAPTER 10

Outsourcing

Outsourcing is a way to improve the effectiveness of an HR function and make it more strategic. Outsourcing transactional work can reduce the administrative workload of HR organizations, increase quality, and reduce costs (Lawler, Ulrich, Fitz-enz, and Madden 2004). By outsourcing professional and knowledge work, organizations can acquire expertise and strategic information that may not be available internally.

In the best-case scenario, transaction outsourcing companies can provide better and cheaper services because they are focused on a particular process or area of expertise that is their core competency. In addition, when they provide transaction services, they can capture economies of scale by servicing multiple organizations. They also can improve the processes of organizations because of the knowledge they have.

At the very least, outsourcing can reduce the number of employees who are on the HR department payroll and can create a flexible cost structure when services are needed occasionally or for short periods of time. They also can allow companies to adjust to economic changes by relatively easily increasing or decreasing the number of people who are working on their HR programs.

The situation with using consultants to provide expertise in areas such as HR strategy, organization development, and training is different. Here the hoped-for advantages are not as much related to scale as they are to expertise. This is particularly true in the case of the large HR consulting firms, which are able to provide a depth of expertise in their areas of specialization that most companies cannot hope to achieve.

Use of Outsourcing

Table 10.1 shows the degree to which nineteen HR activities are currently being outsourced. Activities are grouped by the six factors that our statistical analysis produced; seven items did not group. In 1995, 1998, 2001, 2004, and 2007, the use of outsourcing varied widely among the activities, but in no case were any of these activities even close to being completely outsourced by a majority of the companies.

At one extreme in 2007, over 90 percent of the companies did not outsource HR planning, strategic planning, career planning, and organization design, all areas in which HR can add considerable strategic value and act as a strategic partner. However, as was noted in Chapter 4, they are not all areas in which HR is particularly active (strategic planning

Table 10.1. Outsourcing use

Type of Outsourcing	2007 Percentages			Mean					Correlation with HR Role in Strategy 2007
	Not at All	Partially	Completely	1995	1998	2001	2004	2007	
Overall outsourcing (all items)				—	—	1.4	1.3	**1.4**	**.16**
Planning				—	1.1	1.1	1.1	**1.1**	**−.17[t]**
Human capital forecasting and planning[a]	95.3	4.7	0.0	1.0	1.1	1.0	1.0	**1.0**	**−.12**
Strategic planning	92.4	7.6	0.0	—	1.1	1.1	1.1	**1.1**	**−.15**
Organization design/development				—	1.2	1.2	1.2	**1.1**	**.06**
Organization development	83.0	16.0	0.9	1.3	1.3	1.2	1.2	**1.2[1]**	**.06**
Organization design	93.4	6.6	0.0	—	1.2	1.1	1.1	**1.1**	**.03**
Training				1.6	1.7	1.7	1.7	**1.6**	**.15**
Training and education	26.4	70.8	2.8	1.6	1.9	1.8	1.8	**1.8**	**.23***
Management development	52.8	47.2	0.0	1.5	1.6	1.6	1.6	**1.5**	**.03**
HR information systems	44.8	48.6	6.7	1.3	1.6	1.5	1.5	**1.6[1]**	**.14**
Staffing and career development				1.2	1.2	1.2	1.3	**1.2[1d]**	**.06**
Performance appraisal	83.0	16.0	0.9	1.0	1.1	1.1	1.1	**1.2[1]**	**.09**
Recruitment	45.3	51.9	2.8	1.4	1.6	1.5	1.6	**1.6[1]**	**.12**
Selection	81.1	18.9	0.0	1.2	1.2	1.2	1.2	**1.2**	**−.11**
Career planning	97.2	2.8	0.0	1.1	1.2	1.2	1.1	**1.0[1]**	**−.01**
Metrics				—	—	—	1.2	**1.2**	**.12**
Data analysis and mining	78.8	21.2	0.0	—	—	—	1.2	**1.2**	**.13**
HR metrics	88.6	10.5	1.0	—	—	—	1.2	**1.1**	**.08**
Benefits	14.4	75.0	10.6	1.7	1.9	1.9	2.0	**2.0[1]**	**.16**
Compensation	64.2	35.8	0.0	1.2	1.5	1.5	1.4	**1.4[1]**	**.18[t]**
Legal affairs	53.3	41.9	4.8	1.4	1.6	1.6	1.6	**1.5**	**.12**
Employee assistance	16.0	39.6	44.3	—	2.2	2.3	2.5	**2.3**	**−.03**
Competency/talent assessment	70.5	27.6	1.9	—	—	1.3	1.5	**1.3**	**−.02**
Union relations	90.0	9.0	1.0	1.1	1.1	1.1	1.2	**1.1**	**.03**

[a]"HR planning" prior to 2007

[1]Significant difference ($p \le .05$) between 1995 and 2007.

[d]Means: 1.169 (1995), 1.243 (2007)

Significance level: [t] $p \le .10$; * $p \le .05$; ** $p \le .01$; *** $p \le .001$

and organization design). They do, however, represent areas of opportunity for HR, given their importance.

By a large margin, the most likely area to be completely outsourced is employee assistance, with 44.3 percent of the companies completely outsourcing it in 2007. This is hardly surprising given its personal and confidential nature. Benefits was the next most likely to be outsourced; 85 percent of the companies partially or completely outsourced it. The frequency of outsourcing benefits probably reflects the combination of transactional and specialized knowledge work that it involves. In over 50 percent of companies, training, recruitment, and HRIS were partially or completely outsourced. Management development was partially outsourced by almost 50 percent of the companies.

A relatively new approach to outsourcing involves having a single firm do multiple HR activities (Lawler, Ulrich, Fitz-enz, and Madden 2004). In 2007, we asked for the first time whether the companies had a multiple-process HR outsourcing contract: 21 percent said they did, and another 10 percent said they are considering it. Most had a single multiple-process vendor, but four firms had two or more.

Overall, outsourcing occurs both in areas in which specialized expertise is involved, such as legal affairs, and areas in which primarily transactional work occurs, such as benefits administration. This result provides confirmation that organizations are outsourcing to gain both transactional efficiency and expertise.

A comparison between the 1995 and 2007 results shows a number of areas in which there is a small increase in the use of outsourcing. Specifically, there are statistically significant increases in the use of outsourcing from 1995 to 2007 in the following areas: record keeping, compensation, recruitment, performance appraisal, affirmative action, and legal affairs. Only organizational development and career planning were less likely to be outsourced in 2007 than in 1995.

The comparison between the 2004 and 2007 data shows essentially no change in the frequency of outsourcing. Although outsourcing has increased since 1995, most of that increase took place between 1995 and 1998. Since 1998, our data show little evidence of an increased use of outsourcing; the obvious conclusion at this point is that there is no current trend toward greater use of outsourcing.

Clearly the opportunity exists for more outsourcing to take place, since few companies completely outsource any of their HR activities and many HR activities are barely outsourced. This finding raises the question of whether there will be a significant increase in the amount of outsourcing.

One possibility is that outsourcing will increase because more and more organizations will decide to outsource their HR administration to the growing number of HR business process outsourcing (BPO) firms that exist (Lawler, Ulrich, Fitz-enz, and Madden 2004). However, there is little reason to believe there will be a significant increase in many of the types of outsourcing that are shown in Table 10.1. In many of these areas, knowledge and understanding of an organization's operations are necessary; as a result, they are much less likely to be outsourced than are the kinds of transactional work that are being outsourced to HR BPO firms.

Table 10.1 also shows the relationship between outsourcing and the role that HR plays in strategy. There is little indication that these two issues are related. Only the correlation with training is significant.

Table 10.2 shows that there are very few significant relationships between the strategic focuses and outsourcing. In general, this result is not unexpected, but the lack of a relationship between growth strategies and outsourcing is surprising, especially given our finding in 1998 that growth-focused organizations were more likely to outsource than other organizations. Growth puts a stress on the human resource delivery capabilities of an organization, and outsourcing could provide a quick way to acquire additional support for an HR function that is under pressure to serve a larger organization. It is not clear why this relationship is not present in the 2001, 2004, or 2007 data.

Table 10.2. Relationship of strategic focuses to outsourcing								
	Strategic Focuses							
Type of Outsourcing	Growth	Core Business	Quality and Speed	Information-Based Strategies	Knowledge-Based Strategies	Organizational Performance	Sustainability	Innovation
Overall outsourcing (all items)	−.04	.16	.22*	.24*	.11	.13	.19^t	.12
Planning	−.04	.01	.01	−.02	−.10	−.18^t	−.12	−.04
Organization design/ development	−.00	.11	.17^t	.19^t	.11	.11	.21*	.21*
Training	−.05	.02	.07	.06	−.01	.02	.25**	.05
HR information systems	.13	.12	.23*	.19^t	.04	.19*	.05	.18^t
Staffing and career development	.02	.14	.26**	.27**	.14	.30**	.09	.13
Metrics	−.12	.04	.06	.11	.13	.05	.00	−.06
Benefits	.13	.14	−.02	−.04	.01	−.03	.08	.06
Compensation	.09	.17^t	.24*	.19^t	.08	.21*	.13	.16^t
Legal affairs	−.06	−.05	−.08	−.01	.02	−.14	.09	−.06
Employee assistance	−.09	.10	.00	.06	−.00	−.10	.07	.05
Competency/talent assessment	−.22*	−.03	.11	.16	.10	.05	.07	−.11
Union relations	−.08	.01	−.04	−.02	−.06	−.00	.14	−.06
Significance level: ^{t} $p \leq .10$; * $p \leq .05$; ** $p \leq .01$; *** $p \leq .001$								

There is little relationship between outsourcing and the management approach of the organization. This is not surprising, since the four management approaches do not differ in how appropriate for them outsourcing is.

Impact of HR Outsourcing

In 2007, for the first time, questions were asked about the impact of outsourcing; Table 10.3 presents the results. It seems to have a positive impact in virtually every area. The exception is cost; here, the data suggest it has neither increased nor decreased costs. The most positive responses are to questions concerned with HR being more strategic and a business partner. Apparently, to a limited extent, it does free up HR to be more strategic and perhaps provide HR with the expertise it needs to be a strategic partner. As far as the overall effectiveness of the HR function is concerned, 58 percent of the HR executives surveyed report it has a positive impact; only 11 percent report it has a negative impact, while 31 percent report no change.

The results for companies with multiple-process outsourcing contracts are positive. As expected, companies with multiple outsourcing contracts are more likely to report that they are involved in strategy work. When asked how satisfied they are, 55 percent report they are satisfied, while 24 percent reported they are dissatisfied, a higher dissatisfaction

Table 10.3. Effectiveness of outsourcing HR services							
How has the outsourcing of HR services affected the following?	Greatly Decreased	Decreased	Stayed the Same	Increased	Greatly Increased	Don't Know	Mean
Overall effectiveness of the HR function	1.2	9.5	31.0	52.4	6.0	12.3	3.5
Ability of HR to be a business partner	0	8.3	31.0	52.4	8.3	11.3	3.6
Ability of HR to contribute to business strategy	0	3.7	42.7	47.6	6.1	11.3	3.6
The cost of HR services	0	32.9	40.2	20.7	6.1	12.3	3.0
The quality of HR services	3.6	15.7	34.9	37.3	8.4	11.3	3.3
The value HR adds to the organization	0	7.0	36.0	47.7	9.3	8.5	3.6
Satisfaction of company employees with HR services	1.2	23.8	39.3	26.2	9.5	10.4	3.2
Satisfaction of HR staff	2.4	19.0	34.5	36.9	7.1	10.4	3.3
Commitment of HR staff	1.2	14.1	47.1	27.1	10.6	9.4	3.3
Mining of employee data by HR	0	12.7	60.8	20.3	6.3	15.1	3.2
Time spent on HR strategy	0	4.8	40.5	50.0	4.8	10.4	3.5
Use of metrics by HR	1.3	1.3	54.4	38.0	5.1	15.1	3.4
Time spent on business strategy by HR	0	2.5	43.2	46.9	7.4	12.3	3.6
Availability of HR metrics	0	9.0	46.2	35.9	9.0	15.1	3.4
Use of HR analytic models	1.3	7.9	63.2	23.7	3.9	17.9	3.2

Table 10.4. HR outsourcing approaches						
In general, how effective do you think the following approaches to HR outsourcing are?	Very Ineffective	Ineffective	Neither	Effective	Very Effective	Mean
No outsourcing	38.2	33.3	21.6	6.9	0	**2.0**
Very limited: only a few transactional services (such as payroll)	2.9	20.6	27.5	47.1	2.0	**3.2**
Moderate outsourcing to multiple vendors	0	11.8	28.4	55.9	3.9	**3.5**
Moderate outsourcing to a single vendor	4.0	12.1	36.4	42.4	5.1	**3.3**
Substantial outsourcing to multiple vendors	8.8	30.4	32.4	26.5	2.0	**2.8**
Substantial outsourcing to a single vendor	14.9	27.7	36.6	16.8	4.0	**2.7**

level with outsourcing than exists for the non-HR BPO companies. It is worth noting that two companies reported they are very dissatisfied with their outsourcing relationships. Obviously there are some multiple-process outsourcing relationships that are not going well.

A new question in 2007 asked about the likely effectiveness of different amounts of outsourcing. Table 10.4 presents the results. The clear winner in the opinion of HR executives is moderate outsourcing to either a single vendor or multiple vendors. The worst option is perceived to be no outsourcing. Somewhat surprising is the low rating for substantial outsourcing to a single vendor, given the number of companies in the sample (21 percent) that have tried this arrangement and are happy with it. It is clear that most firms that do not have an HR BPO contract may be a "hard sell" for an industry that is committed to growth.

Conclusion

Overall, there is very little evidence that outsourcing is in a strong growth mode. As a result, organizations may be missing an opportunity to improve the performance of their HR functions. Outsourcing can allow them to access knowledge and expertise that they lack and are not in a good position to develop. They may also be missing a chance to realize economies of scale.

An obstacle to the growth of outsourcing may be the number of problems associated with it, including the apparent difficulty of getting significant cost and quality advantages. The evidence is mixed on whether it helps HR be more of a strategic partner. HR executives say it can, but the amount of it is not correlated with the degree to which HR plays a role in strategy. So far, however, none of the problems with outsourcing have led to it being seen as having a negative impact in any HR performance area. Thus there remains the possibility that outsourcing will grow in the future.

CHAPTER 11

Use of Information Technology

Information technology (IT) is potentially a way to accomplish HR record keeping, HR transactions, and many other administrative tasks more quickly, efficiently, and accurately, thus enabling HR to save money and spend more time on strategic business support. IT can do more than serve as an administrative tool. It can be a way to deliver expert advice to managers and employees in areas such as selection, career development, and compensation. It can also facilitate change efforts by assessing the capabilities of the workforce and by providing information and training that support change. Finally, it can support the development and implementation of business strategy by providing important information about the capabilities and core competencies of the organization, as well as creating transparency with respect to organizational performance.

Level of Use

Table 11.1 shows the state of IT-based human resource processes from 1995 to 2007. In 2004 and again in 2007 around 60 percent of companies were using Human Resource Information Systems (HRISs) for most or all of their human resource processes, a relatively high level of use. Although there is not a significant increase in use from 2004 to 2007 (there is, in fact, a small decrease), there is a significant increase in use from 2001. This is not surprising, particularly in light of the great amount of activity occurring in the HRIS world. In many respects, the increase almost had to occur, given the increased popularity of business software and the fact that the major business software companies have HR applications (for example, SAP, Oracle). It is surprising, given the growth in the use of IT by companies, that there isn't an increase in use from 2004 to 2007.

Table 11.1. State of human resources information system (HRIS)					
	Percentages				
State of Information System	**1995**	**1998**	**2001**	**2004**	**2007**
Little or no information technology/automation present in the HR function	6.3	8.4	8.3	6.1	**7.7**
Some HR processes are information technology based/automated	45.3	40.3	48.3	32.3	**32.0**
Most processes are information technology based/automated but not fully integrated	40.6	42.9	35.9	48.5	**51.5**
Completely integrated HR information technology/automated system	7.8	8.4	7.6	13.1	**8.7**
Mean	3.50	3.50	3.41	3.69	**3.59**
Response scale: 1 = No information technology; 2 = Little information technology; 3 = Some processes integrated; 4 = Most processes integrated; 5 = Completely integrated					

Activities

In 1998, a series of questions on the use of company HRISs was added to our survey in order to obtain a more complete picture of the capabilities and use of the systems. We asked about the degree to which employees and managers could do certain HR tasks via an HRIS. Table 11.2 shows the results for 1998, 2001, and 2004, grouped on the basis of a statistical factor analysis of the questions. Because of survey length limitations, we did not ask this question in 2007, so our discussion will be limited to data collected in previous surveys.

Table 11.2. HRIS activities done by employees or managers			
	Mean[2]		
Activities	**1998**	**2001**	**2004**
Personnel Records	**2.1**	**2.1**	**2.5[1]**
Change benefit coverage	2.2	2.2	2.5[1]
Change address and/or other personal information	2.0	2.1	2.4[1]
Job Information	—	**2.1**	**2.4[1]**
Apply for a job (external applicants)	1.9	2.2	2.5[1]
Apply for a job (internal applicants)	1.5	2.2	2.6[1]
Post job openings	1.5	2.5	2.5
Post personal resume/bio	—	1.5	1.9[1]
Employee Training	—	**1.7**	**1.9[1]**
New hire orientation	—	1.5	1.7[1]
Skills training	—	1.7	1.9[1]
Scheduling training	—	2.0	2.2[1]
Management Tools	—	—	**1.7**
Career development planning	1.4	1.5	1.6[1]
Obtain advice and information on handling personnel issues	1.5	1.5	1.7[1]
Management development training	—	1.5	1.7[1]
Search for employees with specified skills or competencies	—	1.5	1.6
Assess skills/competencies/knowledge	—	—	1.7
Access knowledge communities or experts	—	—	1.5
Access managers tool kit	—	—	1.8
Salary Planning/Administration	**1.9**	**2.0**	**2.1**
Performance Management	**1.5**	**1.9**	**1.9**
Financial Transactions	—	**1.6**	**1.9[1]**

[1] Significant difference ($p \leq .05$) between 2001 and 2004.

[2] Response scale: 1 = Not at all; 2 = Partially; 3 = Completely

Significance level: [t] $p \leq .10$; * $p \leq .05$; ** $p \leq .01$; *** $p \leq .001$

Perhaps the most striking finding is the variation in the extent to which these HR activities are done by employees and managers on HRISs. Posting job openings, applying for a job, making personal information changes, and changing benefit coverage are done completely on HRISs by employees or managers in over 60 percent of the companies. At the other extreme, there are six activities, primarily in the area of management tools, that in 40 percent or more of the companies are not done on HRISs at all.

What most clearly distinguishes the tasks that are done frequently from those that are done infrequently or not at all is the degree to which the activities are transactional. Transactional activities are particularly likely to be done on an HRIS, whereas those involving expert advice and decision making (for example, all the management tool items) are either done not at all or done only partially via an HRIS. The difference in findings between transactional and advice tools is hardly surprising, since transactions are particularly suited to self-service. It takes much more sophisticated software support to offer advice and training, and it often takes much more skilled users.

Since 1998, more and more companies have invested in HR information systems that can perform virtually all the activities in Table 11.2. A comparison between the 2001 and 2004 results show significant increases in the use of HRISs for a wide range of activities. A particularly large increase occurred from 1998 to 2004 in the ability to use HRISs for job information. Apparently, organizations have increasingly adopted the Web as a way to handle the entire job-application and job-posting processes.

There also is evidence of the increased use of HRISs for performance management purposes. This finding may well reflect the use of HRISs for 360-degree appraisals and for the general accumulation of performance data throughout an organization. The emergence of standard modules for such data in the major software packages being sold to organizations may well be driving this increase.

Overall, it is clear that organizations are making greater use of self-service HRISs in the HR function, at least in the number of activities that are carried out on them. There will likely be continued growth both in the areas in which individuals can service themselves via an HRIS and in the number of companies that use such a system.

IT System Effectiveness

Because of the relative newness of HRISs, there is relatively little information available about their overall effectiveness, or about their impact on the effectiveness of organizations and their HR systems. To measure their effectiveness, beginning in 2001 we asked questions about both the effectiveness of HRISs in general and their effectiveness in key areas.

As can be seen in Table 11.3, a statistical factor analysis grouped the outcome questions asked since 2001 into three clusters: employee satisfaction, efficiency, and business effectiveness. The results for items asked for the first time in 2007 about overall effectiveness, human capital decision making, and impact on the business are also shown in Table 11.3.

The HRISs did not receive very high performance ratings on any of the outcomes. The highest ratings are in the areas of speed and employee satisfaction, but even there, the highest-rated item received a rating just

Table 11.3. HRIS outcomes									
HRIS Outcomes	Percentages					Means			Correlation with HR Role in Strategy 2007
	Little or No Extent	Some Extent	Moderate Extent	Great Extent	Very Great Extent	2001	2004	2007	
Overall[a]						**2.8**	**2.9**	**2.8**	**.00**
Employee Satisfaction						**3.5**	**3.5**	**3.4**	**.06**
Satisfy your employees	13.9	29.7	40.6	13.9	2.0	2.4	2.7	**2.6**	−.02
Alienate employees[2]	44.0	33.0	18.0	2.0	3.0	1.4	1.7	**1.9**[1]	−.10
Efficiency						**2.9**	**3.0**	**2.8**	**−.01**
Improve HR services	10.9	20.8	38.6	25.7	4.0	3.0	3.0	**2.9**	.00
Reduce HR transaction costs	12.9	24.8	31.7	26.7	4.0	2.9	3.0	**2.8**	.03
Speed up HR processes	12.9	21.8	26.7	30.7	7.9	3.1	3.2	**3.0**	−.09
Reduce the number of employees in HR	26.7	25.7	29.7	12.9	5.0	2.4	2.6	**2.4**	.03
Business Effectiveness						**2.3**	**2.4**	**2.5**	**−.02**
Provide new strategic information	21.8	28.7	32.7	13.9	3.0	2.1	2.3	**2.5**[1]	.00
Support strategic change	22.8	25.7	35.6	13.9	2.0	2.3	2.4	**2.5**	−.08
Integrate HR processes (e.g., training, compensation)	27.7	22.8	29.7	15.8	4.0	2.4	2.4	**2.5**	.02
Enable Analysis of Organization's Human Capital	18.8	27.7	28.7	21.8	3.0			**2.6**	.03
Measure HR's Impact on the Business	28.7	35.6	18.8	14.9	2.0			**2.3**	−.01
Improve Human Capital Decisions of Managers Outside HR	31.0	22.0	29.0	17.0	1.0			**2.4**	.07
Effective	8.9	20.8	44.6	21.8	4.0			**2.9**	.10

[1] Significant difference ($p <$ = .05) between 2001 and 2007.

[2] Item is reversed in Employee Satisfaction scale.

[a] Includes items from Employee Satisfaction, Efficiency, and Business Effectiveness scales only.

Significance level: [t] $p \le .10$; * $p \le .05$; ** $p \le .01$; *** $p \le .001$

barely above the middle of the rating scale. One positive note in the ratings of effectiveness is that 44 percent of the respondents say that the systems do not alienate their employees. Employee alienation is a concern of some HR professionals, who are apprehensive that the human touch may be replaced by impersonal, automated services.

It is hardly surprising that high ratings come in the efficiency area, since efficiency is an area in which visible gains should be achieved by an IT system. Nevertheless, it is significant that we now have data that confirm that the systems do, to some extent, improve HR services, reduce costs, and increase speed.

The lowest ratings are in business effectiveness and the new survey items related to human capital management and business impact. They have the potential to affect the degree to which HR is a business partner. So far, however, HR executives do not see their HRISs strongly affecting business effectiveness, strategic organizational change, HR's impact on the business, or human capital decision making, perhaps in part due to the newness of the systems and the fact that organizations are just beginning to learn how to use HRISs as a strategic tool.

The four new items do not get particularly high ratings. The overall effectiveness item gets the highest rating, while improving human capital decisions and measuring HR's impact get very low ratings. Overall it is clear that HRISs are not yet doing a good job of providing the information that HR executives need in order to be strategic business partners.

A comparison among the 2001, 2004, and 2007 data shows some positive movement in the ratings of IT-based HR systems. The business effectiveness ratings generally increase, as do employee satisfaction items.

The relationships between the effectiveness of HRISs and the role of HR in strategy are shown in Table 11.3. They are all insignificant. This is a change from 2004, when some were significant. It is not clear why the 2007 data do not show a relationship, but it does bring into question whether effective HR IT systems will lead to HR playing a more important role in strategy.

Only time will tell whether HRISs can make a major contribution to organizational effectiveness, or whether they simply are not capable of making it. As Boudreau and Ramstad (2003) have noted, a decision science for HR remains elusive, yet it is essential for guiding decision makers through the increasingly daunting amount of information available in HR IT systems. They note that having such a decision science is one reason that data systems in finance, marketing, supply chains, and other areas have been so influential. As the HR profession develops a deeper and more precise decision science, HRISs may become more effective.

Strategic Focuses and Management Approach

As we see in Table 11.4, there are a number of significant relationships between HRIS effectiveness and the strategic focuses. Five of the strategic focuses show some significant relationships. The strongest relationship involves organizational performance; the next strongest involve knowledge-based strategies and information-based strategies. These results are not surprising since these strategies are all ones that can be aided by an effective HRIS, and it is hard to see how an HRIS can be highly effective unless it is supporting a clear strategy.

There are only a few significant correlations between the management approach items and the HRIS effectiveness items. High-involvement management is associated with HRIS improving the human capital decisions of managers, once again making the point that HR has a potential positive and important role in high-involvement organization.

Effectiveness and Use

Table 11.5 shows the relationship of HRIS system effectiveness to the degree of information technology use (see Table 11.1). There clearly is a strong relationship here, as there was in 2001 and 2004. Completely integrated HRISs are rated much higher on overall effectiveness, efficiency, and business effectiveness. Less strongly related, but still significantly related, are employee satisfaction and human capital decision making.

The strong relationships to effectiveness undoubtedly reflect the power that integrated systems have. They offer the opportunity to do many

Table 11.4. Relationship of strategic focuses to HRIS outcomes								
	Strategic Focuses							
HRIS Outcomes	**Growth**	**Core Business**	**Quality and Speed**	**Information-Based Strategies**	**Knowledge-Based Strategies**	**Organizational Performance**	**Sustainability**	**Innovation**
Overall (all items)	−.03	.11	.11	.23*	.21*	.33***	.20*	.18^t
Employee satisfaction	−.10	−.12	.06	.23*	.16	.10	.07	−.03
Efficiency	−.01	.10	.03	.16	.10	.19^t	.18^t	.14
Business effectiveness	.01	.06	.18^t	.26**	.23*	.39***	.19^t	.22*
Improve human capital decisions of managers outside HR	−.09	.00	.12	.21*	.24*	.32***	.18^t	.20^t
Effective	−.18^t	.16	.08	.20^t	.23*	.21*	.25**	.07
Significance level: $^t p \le .10$; $* p \le .05$; $** p \le .01$; $*** p \le .001$								

Table 11.5. Relationship of HRIS outcomes to state of HRIS	
HRIS Outcomes	**HRIS State[1]**
Overall (all items)	.48***
Employee satisfaction	.28**
Efficiency	.46***
Business effectiveness	.49***
Improve human capital decisions of managers outside HR	.31**
Effective	.45***

[1]Response Scale:
1. No information technology present
2. Little information technology present in the HR function
3. Some HR processes are information technology based
4. Most processes are information technology based but not fully integrated
5. Completely integrated HR information technology system
Significance level: $^t p \leq .10$; $^* p \leq .05$; $^{**} p \leq .01$; $^{***} p \leq .001$

things with the HRIS, including analyses related to business effectiveness and business strategy. For example, they can make it possible to assess the practicality of a business strategy by determining whether the organization has the capability to execute it. They also can make it possible to determine the impacts of HR programs and to more effectively develop and reward employees.

Conclusion

Our findings bear out that HRISs are most effective at providing transaction tools for HR administration. When combined with our results on usage we can see that HRISs are used most frequently to do the thing that they do best: administration.

Overall the effectiveness results are disappointing. In only a few areas are HRISs rated as more effective in 2007 than they were in 2001. They also are not rated as very effective in an absolute sense. There are many possible reasons for this result, including the fact that they are relatively new and that companies and managers may be just beginning to learn how to utilize them effectively. The technology is advancing rapidly, and many companies may be experiencing difficulties dealing with a technology that is not well developed.

The evidence is quite clear that an HRIS is most effective when it fits the strategy of an organization. They are particularly likely to be perceived as successful in companies with knowledge- and information-based strategies. Perhaps the strongest finding is that the more things an HRIS can do, and the more services it performs, the more effective it is perceived to be.

CHAPTER 12

Human Resource Skills

The skills and knowledge of the members of an organization's HR function are perhaps the most important determinant of what it does and how well it performs (Ulrich, Brockbank, Johnson, Sandholtz, and Younger 2008). Much of the high-value-added work HR does is knowledge work that requires considerable expertise in a wide variety of areas. In today's rapidly changing global economy, the knowledge and skills requirements for the members of an organization's staff functions are continuing to evolve, just as they are for the firm's core business and technical units. Key issues for HR are which skills and what knowledge HR professionals need, and what the current levels of their skills and knowledge are.

Skill Importance

In 2007, for the first time we asked both HR executives and managers to rate the importance of a variety of HR skills and knowledge. Table 12.1 shows the results based on a statistical analysis that yielded five factors and one item. There is some similarity between our factors and the HR competencies Ulrich and his partners identified in their recent study of competencies (Ulrich et al. 2008). However, ours are more focused on the content knowledge needed by HR executives, while theirs include personal traits (for example, "credible activist"), and as a result there are significant differences.

Although there is some variation in how highly they are rated, most of the skills are rated as high in importance by both HR executives and managers. The skills that are rated particularly high by both groups include business understanding and skills having to do with interpersonal dynamics and change management. Managers rate HR technical skills and communication skills highest. HR executives rate business understanding, team skills, and interpersonal skills highest. A few skills are rated higher by HR executives (such as information technology), and a few are rated higher by managers (for example, organization design). However, when we correlated the mean importance given to the skills by HR executives with those given by managers, we found they are strongly related ($r = .85$; $p < .001$). Apparently, HR executives and managers do agree on which skills the HR staff of an organization need to have.

Overall, it is clear that these results support the argument that HR professionals need to have a range of business skills—it is not enough for

Table 12.1. Importance of HR skills

Skills	HR Executive Percentages			Mean	
	Not Important	Somewhat Important	Very Important	HR Executives	Managers
HR Technical Skills				2.7	2.7
HR technical skills	1.0	26.8	72.2	2.7	2.9[1]
Process execution and analysis	2.1	29.2	68.8	2.7	2.5[1]
Interpersonal Dynamics				2.8	2.7[1]
Team skills	0	12.4	87.6	2.9	2.7
Interpersonal skills	0	14.4	85.6	2.9	2.8
Consultation skills	1.0	20.6	78.4	2.8	2.6
Coaching and facilitation	1.0	22.7	76.3	2.8	2.7
Leadership/management	1.0	15.5	83.5	2.8	2.7
Business Partner Skills				2.6	2.5[1]
Business understanding	0	7.2	92.8	2.9	2.8
Strategic planning	0	38.1	61.9	2.6	2.4[1]
Organization design	3.1	53.6	43.3	2.4	2.7[1]
Change management	0	20.6	79.4	2.8	2.8
Cross-functional experience	8.2	51.5	40.2	2.3	2.2
Global understanding	18.6	39.2	42.3	2.2	2.2
Communications	0	19.6	80.4	2.8	2.9
Metrics Skills				2.4	2.2[1]
Information technology	9.3	55.7	35.1	2.3	2.0[1]
Metrics development	5.2	48.5	46.4	2.4	2.4
Data analysis and mining	6.2	48.5	45.4	2.4	2.3
Managing Contractors/Vendors	12.4	58.8	28.9	2.2	2.1

[1] Significant difference ($p \leq .05$) between HR executives and managers.

them to just be good HR technicians. They need to understand the business and what makes it effective. Further, they need to be able to help design the organization, develop teams and leaders, and support change efforts.

Table 12.2 shows the relationships between skill importance and the strategic focuses. There are a number of significant positive correlations. Two skill areas stand out because they are strongly correlated with most focuses. Business partner skills are significantly correlated with four of the eight, while metrics skills are correlated with five of the eight. It is clear that having these skills is important in organizations that have a well-defined strategic focus.

Table 12.2. Relationship of strategic focuses to importance of HR skills

Importance of the Following	Strategic Focuses							
	Growth	Core Business	Quality and Speed	Information-Based Strategies	Knowledge-Based Strategies	Organizational Performance	Sustainability	Innovation
HR technical skills	.06	.18^t	.08	.19^t	.02	.15	.17^t	.19^t
Interpersonal dynamics	.05	.22*	.01	.09	-.04	–.11	.09	.14
Business partner skills	.40***	.34***	.20^t	.22*	.02	.19^t	.10	.36***
Metrics skills	.18^t	.14	.32***	.33***	.24*	.18^t	.23*	.38***
Managing contractors and vendors	.06	.30**	.05	.14	.01	.16	.20*	.05

Significance level: $^t p \leq .10$; $^* p \leq .05$; $^{**} p \leq .01$; $^{***} p \leq .001$

With one exception, skill importance is not related to the management approach taken in organizations. The only statistically significant relationship is a positive one between business partner skills and the global-competitor management approach.

Skill Satisfaction

Table 12.3 shows the level of satisfaction with the skills of the HR staff as rated by HR executives. Not surprisingly, one of the highest levels of satisfaction is with HR technical skills. The other highest level of satisfaction is with skills that pertain to interpersonal dynamics, including interpersonal skills, team skills, consulting, coaching, and leadership and management skills. This is the only area in which all the individual skills show an increased level of satisfaction when the 2007 data are compared to the 1995 data. Business understanding is the only other individual skill that shows a significant increase in satisfaction.

The highest level of skills satisfaction overall is with interpersonal skills. In some respects this is a positive, but it may reflect HR being an eager-to-please "nice guy" when it could add more value by being an effective business partner and/or metrics expert.

There is a low level of satisfaction with HR staff skills in managing contractors and vendors. This is a skill that has increased in importance in today's world, where outsourcing is central to being able to carry out the HR role.

Another relatively low area of satisfaction is business partner skills. There has been a significant increase in business understanding. However, deficits are still perceived in the substantive business support areas of strategic planning and organization design, and global understanding. As already mentioned, HR staff members usually have low levels of

Table 12.3. Satisfaction with skills of HR staff

Skills	2007 Percentages					Mean				
	Very Dissatisfied	Dissatisfied	Neutral	Satisfied	Very Satisfied	1995	1998	2001	2004	**2007**
HR Technical Skills						—	—	—	3.8	**3.6**
HR technical skills	0	11.3	20.6	50.5	17.5	—	—	—	4.0	**3.7**
Process execution and analysis	2.1	11.3	38.1	41.2	7.2	—	—	—	3.5	**3.4**
Interpersonal Dynamics						3.2	3.1	3.6	3.7	**3.6[1]**
Team skills	0	14.3	17.3	53.1	15.3	3.3	3.2	3.7	3.7	**3.7[1]**
Interpersonal skills	1.0	1.0	18.4	54.1	25.5	3.7	3.5	4.0	4.1	**4.0[1]**
Consultation skills	4.1	16.3	29.6	42.9	7.1	3.0	2.9	3.4	3.4	**3.3[1]**
Coaching and facilitation	1.0	11.2	32.7	40.8	14.3	3.2	3.1	3.4	3.5	**3.6[1]**
Leadership/management	2.0	12.2	33.7	41.8	10.2	3.1	2.9	3.3	3.5	**3.5[1]**
Business Partner Skills						—	—	—	3.2	**3.1**
Business understanding	2.0	20.4	29.6	38.8	9.2	3.0	2.9	3.3	3.3	**3.3[1]**
Strategic planning	7.2	25.8	44.3	18.6	4.1	—	2.8	2.9	3.0	**2.9**
Organization design	4.1	24.5	41.8	27.6	2.0	—	2.7	2.9	3.1	**3.0**
Change management	4.1	20.4	34.7	37.8	3.1	—	—	3.2	3.3	**3.2**
Cross-functional experience	5.1	34.7	35.7	21.4	3.1	2.9	2.8	2.9	2.9	**2.8**
Global understanding	6.2	29.9	43.3	19.6	1.0	—	2.6	2.7	2.8	**2.8**
Communications	1.0	8.2	27.8	49.5	13.4	—	—	—	3.8	**3.7**
Metrics Skills						—	—	—	2.8	**2.7**
Information technology	11.2	20.4	45.9	16.3	6.1	—	—	3.1	3.0	**2.9**
Metrics development	10.2	38.8	31.6	14.3	5.1	—	—	—	2.7	**2.7**
Data analysis and mining	19.4	39.8	22.4	11.2	7.1	—	—	—	2.8	**2.5**
Managing Outsourcing						—	—	3.4	3.5	**3.4**
Managing contractors and vendors	2.1	13.4	35.1	40.2	9.3	—	3.2	3.3	3.3	**3.4**
Record keeping	—	—	—	—	—	3.6	3.6	3.7	3.7	**—**

Items with means indicated by (—) were not asked.

[1] Significant difference ($p \leq .05$) between 1995 and 2007.

cross-functional experience, a factor that may well contribute to relatively low scores in the business partner area.

Although HR professionals may increasingly understand the business, they still do not appear to bring substantive business expertise to the table. This deficit clearly has to change if HR is to influence an organization's strategic and organizational direction. It is a critical weakness with respect to HR's performing as an effective business partner. Fixing this deficit requires going well beyond learning simple business acumen or taking finance and marketing classes. A comprehensive perspective on strategy through the lens of HR and human capital needs to be understood by HR professionals.

As in 2004, the lowest satisfaction level is with metrics and information technology skills. HR managers need to greatly improve their skills in this area. The areas of metrics development and data analysis and mining even show a slight decrease in satisfaction from their levels of satisfaction in 2004. Metrics skills are particularly critical in terms of the ability of the HR function to play a major business strategy role. Understanding data and performing data analyses are critical in many business decisions; thus it is particularly important that HR executives have good skills in these areas.

Table 12.4 compares the skill satisfaction responses of HR executives with those of other managers. It yields a rather surprising result: in most skill areas, HR executives are actually less satisfied with the skills of the HR staff than are other managers. The two exceptions here are managing contractors and communications. Interestingly, this trend was also found in our 2004 survey, which was the first survey that gathered data from managers on skill satisfaction. We have no survey data that identify the cause of this pattern, but it may be that HR suffers from a bit of an inferiority complex because it is often on the defensive and criticized by others within the organization and in the press.

The differences between the views of HR executives and managers are particularly striking in the area of metrics. As in 2004, managers rate HR staff as significantly more skillful vis-à-vis metrics development and data analysis and mining than do HR executives. We suspect that this result may arise in part because managers have low expectations and may be impressed with the mere existence of measures, data, and scorecards. HR executives, in contrast, may be better able to see the untapped potential in such systems. Other areas in which major rating differences appear include organization design, change management, and global understanding.

Four of the business partner skill areas are rated lower by HR executives than by managers. This appears to be one area in which HR underestimates its skills. What may need to happen for HR to become more of a business partner is for it to realize that it often has something to contribute in this area and that others see it as capable of adding value. Perhaps it needs to knock on the business partner door more often; our data suggest that if it does, it is likely to find a more favorable reception than it expects.

Despite the fact that HR executives and managers differ in how satisfied they are with certain HR skills, they are in general agreement when it

Table 12.4. Satisfaction with skills and knowledge of HR staff				
	HR Executives		**Managers**	
Skills	**Mean**	**Correlation with HR Role in Strategy**	**Mean**	**Correlation with HR Role in Strategy**
HR Technical Skills	**3.6**	**.25***	**3.8[1]**	**.58*****
HR technical skills	3.7	.15	4.3[1]	.38*
Process execution and analysis	3.4	.31**	3.6	.64***
Interpersonal Dynamics	**3.6**	**.41*****	**3.9[1]**	**.51*****
Team skills	3.7	.23*	4.0[1]	.43**
Interpersonal skills	4.0	.43***	4.3	.40*
Consultation skills	3.3	.33***	3.8[1]	.40**
Coaching and facilitation	3.6	.22*	3.8	.49***
Leadership/management skills	3.5	.37***	3.7	.44**
Business Partner Skills	**3.1**	**.38*****	**3.4[1]**	**.67*****
Business understanding	3.3	.27**	3.6	.39*
Strategic planning	2.9	.34***	3.4[1]	.63***
Organization design	3.0	.25*	3.7[1]	.72***
Change management	3.2	.39***	3.5	.54***
Cross-functional experience	2.8	.27**	3.1[1]	.56***
Global understanding	2.8	.14	3.2[1]	.39*
Communications	3.7	.33***	3.7	.59***
Metrics Skills	**2.7**	**.18[t]**	**3.1[1]**	**.62*****
Information technology	2.9	.11	3.2	.36*
Metrics development	2.7	.21*	3.2[1]	.66***
Data analysis and mining	2.5	.15	3.3[1]	.45**
Managing Contractors and Vendors	**3.4**	**.11**	**3.2**	**.39***

Response scale: 1 = Very dissatisfied; 2 = Dissatisfied; 3 = Neither; 4 = Satisfied; 5 = Very satisfied

[1] Significant difference ($p \leq .05$) between HR executives and managers

Significance level: [t] $p \leq .10$; * $p \leq .05$; ** $p \leq .01$; *** $p \leq .001$

comes to which skills they are most and least satisfied with. When we correlated the mean satisfaction levels for managers and HR executives, we found a very high correlation ($r = .88$; $p < .001$). Thus it seems HR executives and managers are in general agreement about what HR can do well and what it cannot do well.

Role in Strategy

The relationship between HR skill satisfaction and HR's role in strategy is shown in Table 12.4. Let's look first at the correlations for the HR executives' data. As in 2004, the correlations for HR technical skills, interpersonal dynamics, and business partner skills are mostly high and statistically significant. Metrics skills and managing vendors are less strongly related to HR's role in strategy.

The correlations between HR technical skills and the role in strategy support the view that HR technical skills are required in order for HR to be involved in business strategy. The correlations between interpersonal dynamics and business partner skills were expected to be high, given that they are truly the foundation for contributing to business strategy from both an implementation and a development point of view. It is surprising that the correlations between metrics skills and HR's role in strategy are so low. These skills certainly are potentially useful in strategy development and implementation.

A somewhat different picture of the relationship of HR skills and HR's role in strategy exists in the data from managers. All the skills areas are significantly related to managers' perceptions of HR's role in strategy. This suggests that HR technical mastery is important to being involved with strategy. Perhaps it is a way to establish credibility. Not surprisingly, business partner skills are significantly related to managers' perceptions of HR being involved with strategy. Metrics skills also are strongly related to HR's role in strategy. This result is more understandable than the result of no relationship between them in the answers by HR managers.

Overall, our findings about the relationship between skill satisfaction and the strategic role of HR strongly suggest that organizational dynamics skills and business partner skills are critical to being a business partner. Less important—at least in the findings for HR executives—but still relevant are HR technical skills and metrics skills.

Overall Skill Levels

Despite the improvement in satisfaction with skills in some areas, as we see in Table 12.5, the percentage of HR professionals with the necessary overall skills has not changed significantly from 1995 to 2007 in the judgment of HR executives and managers. Very few HR executives report that over 80 percent of their staff have the necessary skills. The same conclusion is reached by the line managers, who give a slightly lower appraisal of the skills of HR professionals.

One explanation for the low overall skill ratings of HR professionals is that the areas of low skill satisfaction shown in Table 12.3 are viewed as very important in the overall skill portfolio of the HR function. Thus, although skill development progress is being made in the traditional areas of HR expertise and in organizational dynamics, many HR professionals have not yet developed all the important skills they need.

Table 12.5. HR professionals with skill set							
Have Skills	**Percentages**						
	1995	1998	2001	2004		2007	
				HR Executives	Managers	HR Executives	Managers
None	0	0	0	0	0	0	0
1–20%	0	2	5	2	5	2	5
21–40%	19	15	19	12	17	17	15
41–60%	35	39	33	37	28	34	25
61–80%	37	40	33	34	37	37	53
81–99%	9	4	10	11	13	10	3
100%	1	0	0	3	0	0	0
Mean	**4.4**	**4.3**	**4.3**	**4.5**	**4.3**	**4.4**	**4.3**

Response scale: 1 = None; 2 = 1–20%; 3 = 21–40%; 4 = 41–60%; 5 = 61–80%; 6 = 81–99%; 7 = 100%

Table 12.6. Relationship of strategic focuses to HR skills satisfaction								
Skills Satisfaction	**Strategic Focuses**							
	Growth	Core Business	Quality and Speed	Information-Based Strategies	Knowledge-Based Strategies	Organizational Performance	Sustainability	Innovation
HR technical skills	–.02	.01	–.03	.07	.15	.00	.19^t	–.03
Interpersonal dynamics	.02	.14	.17	.12	.25*	.17^t	.25*	.08
Business partner skills	.09	.21*	.15	.24*	.18^t	.27**	.27**	.11
Metrics skills	.01	.13	.09	.23*	.22*	.31**	.32***	.12
Managing contractors and vendors	.11	.10	.12	.22*	.05	.16	.25*	–.04

Significance level: ^{t} $p \leq .10$; * $p \leq .05$; ** $p \leq .01$; *** $p \leq .001$

Strategic Focuses

The relationship between the strategic focuses and HR skills satisfaction as rated by HR executives is shown in Table 12.6. There are a number of positive correlations, particularly with respect to business partner skills, metrics skills, and interpersonal dynamics skills. They are all associated with three or more of the strategic focuses.

Overall, organizations with stronger strategic focuses tend to have HR functions with better skill sets (most of the correlations in Table 12.6 are positive). This seems to be particularly true of organizations that have organizational performance, sustainability, knowledge-based, and information-based strategic focuses. It is easy to see why the knowledge and organizational performance focuses would lead to better skills in the

HR area. They often require HR functions that are able not only to execute their technical skills but to design systems that support organizational performance and knowledge development and utilization.

The relationship of the sustainability focus to skills satisfaction is particularly interesting. It has the largest number of significant correlations. One possible explanation for this is that sustainability is a strategy that more developed and sophisticated organizations adopt, and that this type of organization is likely to have a well-developed HR organization. Alternatively, it may be that because they have a focus of sustainability, organizations develop their HR organizations. The third alternative explanation, that because they have a skilled HR function they adopt a sustainability strategy, seems less likely, but it is possible.

As was true with skill importance, there is only one significant relationship between a management approach and skills satisfaction. It is a negative one between interpersonal dynamics skills and being a low-cost operator. Low-cost operators have a low level of satisfaction with the interpersonal dynamics skills of their HR function. This is not surprising, given that in most low-cost-operator organizations, HR is primarily an administrative unit and indeed is often in the position of communicating bad news and enforcing rules and regulations.

Conclusion

The results suggest that HR suffers from a skills deficit. It is notable that there is generally only moderate satisfaction with all HR skills (no rating by HR executives was higher than 3.7 on a 5-point scale), and that most ratings fall around the neutral point. Of particular concern are the relatively low ratings given to business partner skills, since they are related to HR playing a significant role in strategy. On the encouraging side, there has been an improvement in interpersonal dynamics skills. Still, there is much work to be done on enhancing HR skills, as well as developing a common understanding about the level those skills need to be at in order for the HR organization to be effective.

CHAPTER 13

Effectiveness of the HR Organization

The overall effectiveness of an HR organization must be determined on the basis of an assessment of its performance in a number of areas. The most obvious area is service delivery, but good service delivery is not enough. To be an effective business partner, HR has to support current business performance by contributing to effective employment relationships and good staffing and training decisions. To operate effectively as a strategic partner, it needs to deliver value with respect to business strategy, organizational change, and human capital decision making. How is HR doing? To answer this question, we have included items in all our surveys that ask about HR performance.

HR Effectiveness

HR executives and managers were asked to judge the overall effectiveness of their HR organizations and to judge their effectiveness in thirteen activities. As shown in Table 13.1, our statistical analysis produced three groups of effectiveness items: corporate activities, services, and business and strategy.

The results for HR executives show higher ratings for 2004 than for 1995, 1998, and 2001. But the 2007 results show a decline from the 2004 level (all items are rated lower), although many of the ratings are still higher than they were in 1998; five of the activities are rated higher in 2007. It is not clear why this recent decline has occurred. At the very least it is a strong indicator that HR performance is not improving in the opinion of HR executives.

The results for managers are mixed. Some 2007 ratings are higher (five items) than those in 2004; some are lower (five items). The rest are the same (three items). This too suggests that there has been no overall increase in the performance of HR.

The effectiveness ratings from 1985, 1998, 2001, 2004, and 2007 are highest for the HR services area. This is true of the ratings by both HR executives and managers. The highest-rated item in the survey is providing HR services. Also highly rated is being an employee advocate. This finding is consistent with other studies, which have found that HR tends to be rated particularly highly when it comes to the delivery of basic HR services (Csoka and Hackett 1998).

HR receives its lowest ratings when it comes to the business and strategy area. Both HR executives and managers rate activities in this area

Table 13.1. Effectiveness of HR organization	1995	1998	2001	2004		2007			
				HR Executives	Managers	HR Executives		Managers	
Activities				Mean	Mean	Mean	Correlation with HR Role in Strategy	Mean	Correlation with HR Role in Strategy
Overall Effectiveness (All Items)				**6.9**	**6.7**	**6.4**	**.46*** **	**6.5**	**.75*** **
HR Services				**7.0**	**6.8**	**6.7**	**.39*** **	**6.9**	**.67*** **
Providing HR services	7.2	7.0	7.3	7.8	7.2[1]	7.4[2]	.33***	7.6	.36*
Tailoring human resource practices to fit business needs	6.9	6.9	6.7	7.1	6.4[1]	6.7	.31**	6.9	.54***
Helping shape a viable employment relationship for the future	—	5.8	6.4	6.9	6.5	6.6[2]	.33***	6.8	.56***
Being an employee advocate	—	6.8	7.2	7.4	7.3	7.3[2]	.24*	7.6	.62***
Analyzing HR and business metrics	—	—	—	5.9	6.4	5.3	.32**	6.1[1]	.68***
Corporate Roles				**6.9**	**6.8**	**6.5**	**.37*** **	**6.1**	**.70*** **
Managing outsourcing	—	—	—	—	—	6.1	.12	6.2	.25
Operating HR centers of excellence	—	5.5	5.6	6.8	6.0[1]	6.7[2]	.26*	5.9	.50**
Operating HR shared service units	—	5.7	6.0	6.9	6.5	6.3[2]	.19[t]	6.5	.29
Working with the corporate board	—	—	—	7.1	7.1	6.8	.48***	6.4	.68***
Business and Strategy				**6.5**	**6.3**	**6.1**	**.49*** **	**6.3**	**.78*** **
Providing change consulting services	5.8	5.5	5.7	6.5	6.1	5.9	.34***	6.0	.63***
Being a business partner	6.3	6.5	6.4	7.1	6.8	6.8	.49***	7.2	.77***
Helping to develop business strategies	—	6.2	5.8	6.0	5.7	5.8	.55***	5.5	.71***
Improving decisions about human capital	—	—	—	6.7	6.7	6.1	.33***	6.7	.73***
Overall Performance	—	—	—	**7.2**	**6.7**	**6.7**	**.47*** **	**7.2**	**.67*** **

Response scale: 1 = Not meeting needs, 10 = All needs met

Items with means indicated by (—) were not asked.

[1] Significant difference ($p \leq .05$) between HR executives and managers.

[2] Significant difference ($p \leq .05$) between 1998 and 2007.

Significance level: [t] $p \leq .10$; * $p \leq .05$; ** $p \leq .01$; *** $p \leq .001$

the lowest in effectiveness. The ratings by both HR executives and managers are lowest for the developing business strategy activity. However, being a business partner is rated relatively high. This finding supports the point made in Chapter 1 that there is a difference between being a business partner and having an active role in strategy development. When managers and HR executives consider a successful business partnership, they don't seem to see it as synonymous with an active role in developing business strategies.

The ratings by HR executives and managers of HR's performance in its corporate roles are mixed. HR gets low ratings on managing outsourcing; it gets higher ratings on work with the board.

A comparison of the ratings in 2007 by HR executives and those by managers shows some differences and a trend. Managers rate HR more highly on nine of thirteen activities and on overall performance. This is a bit surprising. It wasn't true in 2004; then, managers rated HR lower than HR executives did on all but two activities.

It may be that HR executives are increasingly aware of what it means to be an effective HR function and are raising the performance bar. It's also possible that HR underrates its performances, possibly as a result of its being criticized by managers and the press.

Although there is a general trend for HR executives to give lower ratings, there is a high level of agreement between HR executives and managers on which activities HR performs well and poorly. The mean ratings of performance by HR executives correlate highly with those by managers ($r = .78, p < .001$). This is a positive for HR, since it means that it is not at odds with the rest of the organization when it comes to opinions about how well it is performing.

To better understand the overall performance ratings HR executives and managers gave to the HR function, we analyzed these ratings further. We did a regression analysis to see how their ratings of specific activities were related to their ratings of overall performance.

For HR executives, the most important determinant of their overall rating is their rating of HR's performance in delivering services. Next in line is change consulting services. Very different results were obtained for managers. For them, the best predictors are being a business partner and developing business strategies. Put together, these findings suggest that when it comes to performance, HR executives think of how HR does as a service deliverer, while managers think of how it does as a business partner. One implication of this is that in order to be seen by others as a good performer, HR needs to perform better as a strategic partner, which is a relatively low performance area for it.

One final way to look at the ratings on effectiveness concerns their absolute level. The ratings are on a 10-point scale; thus even the highest ratings, 7.4 for HR executives and 7.6 for managers, fall significantly short of the top of the scale. Clearly, there is still plenty of room for HR to improve its effectiveness, particularly in those activities that are related to the business and strategy.

Role in Strategy

Table 13.1 also shows the correlations between the role that HR plays in strategy and its effectiveness. There are a number of high correlations here, with respect to the data from both the HR executives and the managers. Not surprisingly, the strongest pattern of relationships has to do with the effectiveness of HR performance in the business and strategy area. The more effective HR is in this area, the more it plays an active role in strategy formulation. The implication of this is clear: if HR wants to play a more important role in strategy formulation, it needs to be more effective when it comes to the business and strategy activities shown in Table 13.1. This is the area of lowest performance, so there is plenty of room for improvement.

In the data from both HR executives and managers, effectiveness in providing HR services is significantly related to the strategic role of HR. It is impossible to tell from the data whether the correlations with service effectiveness mean that providing good services is a prerequisite to playing a strategic role or that HR organizations that are doing a good job at service delivery are also partners in strategy for another reason.

The results with respect to corporate roles have some of the lowest and highest correlations with HR's role in strategy. Effectively working with corporate boards and operating centers of excellence is strongly related to being a strategic partner for both HR executives and managers, but managing outsourcing and shared service centers is not.

The Importance of HR Performance

The results for the ratings of the importance of HR performance in Table 13.2 show generally high ratings in both the 2004 and 2007 data (asked for the first time in 2004). Both HR executives and managers see overall HR performance as very important. The highest 2007 importance ratings for HR managers concern improving decisions about human capital, being a business partner, and providing HR services.

The lowest ratings by both HR executives and managers are given to the corporate roles items. It is interesting that both HR executives and managers rate providing HR services very highly. This finding once again makes the point that HR must not lose sight of the importance of delivering basic HR services.

Table 13.2. Importance of HR performance

Activities	2004 HR Executives Mean	2004 Managers Mean	2007 HR Executives Mean	2007 HR Executives Correlation with HR Role in Strategy	2007 Managers Mean	2007 Managers Correlation with HR Role in Strategy
Overall Importance (All Items)	**8.1**	**8.0**	**8.1**	**.20[t]**	**7.9**	**.50*****
HR Services	**8.3**	**8.4**	**8.1**	**.08**	**8.3**	**.23**
Providing HR services	9.0	8.8	8.5	−.14	9.3[1]	.13
Tailoring human resource practices to fit business needs	8.4	8.5	8.2	.21*	8.7	.18
Helping shape a viable employment relationship for the future	8.6	8.6	8.4	.13	8.3	.15
Being an employee advocate	7.9	7.9	7.5	.02	7.8	.05
Analyzing HR and business metrics	7.9	8.1	8.2	.08	7.8	.40*
Corporate Roles	**7.6**	**7.5**	**7.3**	**.20***	**7.2**	**.53*****
Managing outsourcing	—	—	6.6	.08	6.9	.06
Operating HR centers of excellence	7.7	7.6	7.9	.07	7.3	.56***
Operating HR shared service units	7.6	7.4	7.4	.07	7.4	.29
Working with the corporate board	8.0	8.0	7.2	.28**	7.1	.38*
Business and Strategy	**8.4**	**8.2**	**8.7**	**.20***	**8.0[1]**	**.45****
Providing change consulting services	8.2	8.1	8.3	.08	7.8	.13
Being a business partner	9.0	8.7	9.1	.19[t]	8.7	.48**
Helping to develop business strategies	8.0	7.3[1]	8.4	.14	7.3[1]	.39*
Improving decisions about human capital	8.3	8.8[1]	8.8	.22*	8.7	.47**
Overall Performance	**8.9**	**8.8**	**9.1**	**.03**	**8.6[1]**	**.36***

Response scale: 1 = Not important, 10 = Very important

Note: Items with means indicated by (—) were not asked.

[1]Significant difference ($p \le .05$) between HR executives and managers.

Significance level: [t] $p \le .10$; * $p \le .05$; ** $p \le .01$; *** $p \le .001$

There are two items for which there is a significant disagreement between HR executives and managers. HR executives attach more importance than managers to developing business strategies, while managers put more importance on providing HR services. For managers, HR developing business strategies is rated as one of the lowest areas in importance. This result reinforces the pattern we saw earlier: business leaders value more highly HR's contribution to decisions about human capital and its service provision than they do its developing business strategies; HR executives, however, see them as almost equally important. One implication of this pattern is that HR leaders may need to do some selling to the non-HR community with respect to what they can contribute to business strategy.

As for the correlations between HR's role in strategy and the HR activity importance ratings, a number of items are statistically significant, but the correlations are not high. The majority of the strongest relationships involve responses from managers. Not surprisingly, playing a major role in strategy is associated with placing high importance on the various corporate roles and on the business and strategy items. This is particularly true for managers; those who feel it is important for HR to play a corporate role and to be involved in the business report that HR is more involved in strategy. In this case, it may well be that the reason HR is involved in strategy is because managers see the importance of HR performance in these areas.

Effectiveness and Importance

The results of a comparison between the importance ratings assigned to HR activities and their effectiveness ratings are shown in Table 13.3. To create this table, the effectiveness ratings were subtracted from the importance ratings. Thus the larger the number, the bigger the gap

Table 13.3. HR importance and effectiveness rating differences		
	HR Executives	**Managers**
Activities	**Means***	**Means***
Overall Importance/Effectiveness (All Items)	**1.6**	**1.4**
HR Services	**1.5**	**1.4**
Providing HR services	1.0	1.6
Tailoring human resource practices to fit business needs	1.5	1.8
Helping shape a viable employment relationship for the future	1.8	1.5
Being an employee advocate	0.1	0.2
Analyzing HR and business metrics	2.9	1.6
Corporate Roles	**0.7**	**1.1**
Managing outsourcing	0.5	0.8
Operating HR centers of excellence	1.2	1.6
Operating HR shared-services units	1.1	1.2
Working with the corporate board	0.5	0.6
Business and Strategy	**2.5**	**1.7**
Providing change-consulting services	2.3	1.8
Being a business partner	2.3	1.5
Helping to develop business strategies	2.6	1.8
Improving decisions about human capital	2.8	2.1
*Mean difference between Importance and Effectiveness ratings for each activity. Importance response scale: 1 = Not important; 10 = Very important Effectiveness response scale: 1 = Not meeting needs; 10 = All needs met		

between importance and effectiveness and the greater the cause for concern, because it means HR is doing an important thing poorly.

The results for HR executives and managers are relatively similar. For both groups, most of the largest numbers are in the business and strategy area. The one outlier is analyzing HR and business metrics. It shows the largest difference for HR executives, but doesn't have a particularly large difference in the case of managers. This may well be due to HR having a better understanding of what can be done and isn't being done in this area.

Both managers and HR executives show small gaps in the case of being an employee advocate. It is not surprising that managers feel this way. They are known to complain that HR sometimes is too much of an employee advocate. Perhaps HR has gotten the message, since there is only a small gap here for HR executives.

Finally, it is interesting that there is a very small gap for corporate boards. This is an important area in which it often seems HR could do much more and be more effective. Apparently that is not the way HR executives and managers see things.

Conclusion

HR executives and other managers seem to be in general agreement about where HR is effective. Both say it has been particularly effective at delivering HR services. It also appears that HR has improved its effectiveness since 1995. However, delivering HR services is not seen by HR executives as its most important contribution area. The most important area, according to HR executives, is business and strategy.

HR executives say that a strong emphasis needs to be placed on HR's role as a business partner and on improving decisions about human capital. These are areas of relatively low effectiveness for HR, and thus there is a tremendous opportunity for improvement on the part of HR. They are also areas that are related to the strategic involvement of the HR function. Thus, by making improvements in these areas, HR is likely to become much more of a strategic partner.

CHAPTER 14

Determinants of HR Effectiveness

What determines how effective an HR organization is? To answer this question, we need to look at the relationship between the effectiveness of the HR organization and the HR practices and activities that are likely to influence its effectiveness.

Time Spent

As we saw in Chapter 3, the amount of time spent on the major HR roles has not changed much over the past twelve years. Yet the amount of time spent on two roles relates significantly to HR effectiveness. As can be seen in Table 14.1, our results show a strong negative relationship between effectiveness and the amount of time the HR function spends maintaining records. There is a significant positive relationship between spending time as a strategic business partner and HR effectiveness. These results are consistent with what we found in the 2004 survey as well.

The positive correlation between time spent on being a business partner and HR effectiveness is consistent with the positive correlation between HR effectiveness and the role HR plays in strategy, as reported in Chapter 13. The more HR is involved in business strategy, the more effective HR is seen to be, a relationship that is significant for HR executive ratings and for managers (see Table 13.1).

Table 14.1. Relationship of HR roles (time spent) and HR effectiveness		
	HR Executives' Rating of HR Effectiveness[1]	
Roles[2]	2004	2007
Maintaining Records Collect, track, and maintain data on employees	–.47***	–.38***
Auditing and Controlling Ensure compliance to internal operations, regulations, and legal and union requirements	–.04	–.13
Human Resources Service Provider Assist with implementation and administration of HR practices	–.04	–.01
Development of Human Resources Systems and Practices Develop new HR systems and practices	.25[t]	.02
Strategic Business Partner Member of the management team; involved with strategic HR planning, organizational design, and strategic change	.29*	.34***
[1] Based on total score for all thirteen effectiveness items as rated by HR executives. [2] Based on percentage of time spent on HR roles as rated by HR executives. Significance level: [t] $p \leq .10$; * $p \leq .05$; ** $p \leq .01$; *** $p \leq .001$		

The negative correlation between time spent on maintaining records and effectiveness is consistent with the findings indicating that self-service HR systems are associated with HR's strategic role and its effectiveness. Our findings paint a consistent picture suggesting that effective HR organizations are evolving away from spending time on labor-intensive data and record-keeping activities, and becoming more involved in human-capital and business-strategy issues.

It is interesting that in Table 14.1 only the two "extreme" roles are significantly related to HR effectiveness. The other roles, auditing and controlling, providing services, and developing HR systems, are neither positively nor negatively related to HR effectiveness. This suggests that for these roles, the association with HR effectiveness may be more situationally specific, in that their contribution to effectiveness depends on the nature of the organization and the role of the HR function.

HR Strategy

HR's role in the strategy process is very strongly related to the effectiveness of the HR function, as shown in Table 14.2. Indeed, when compared to the 2004 results, the relationships in 2007 are even stronger and more consistent. In 2007, all but one of the correlations are statistically significant. The biggest difference between 2004 and 2007 seems to be for the manager sample, for which the absolute level of the correlations is consistently higher in 2007 than in 2004.

Table 14.2. Relationship of business strategy activities to HR effectiveness				
	HR Effectiveness			
	2004		2007	
Strategy Activities Done by HR	HR Executives[1]	Managers[2]	HR Executives[1]	Managers[2]
Help identify or design strategy options	.27^t	.32*	**.36***	**.46**
Help decide among the best strategy options	.40**	.39**	**.39***	**.56***
Help plan the implementation of strategy	.28*	.24^t	**.39***	**.46**
Help identify new business opportunities	.23^t	.39**	**.27**	**.53***
Assess the organization's readiness to implement strategies	.25^t	.30*	**.39***	**.53***
Help design the organization structure to implement strategy	.38**	.38**	**.40***	**.58***
Assess possible merger, acquisition, or divestiture strategies	.22	.25^t	**.24***	**.52***
Work with the corporate board on business strategy	.27^t	.29*	**.25***	**.56***
Recruit and develop talent	.29*	.37**	**.19^t**	**.74***
[1] Based on total score for all thirteen effectiveness items as rated by HR executives.				
[2] Based on total score for all thirteen effectiveness items as rated by managers.				
Significance level: ^{t} $p \leq .10$; * $p \leq .05$; ** $p \leq .01$; *** $p \leq .001$				

There is one item for which we see a particularly large difference between managers and HR executives. For managers in 2007, by far the highest correlation with HR effectiveness is for the "recruit and develop talent" role. For the HR sample in 2007, this is the lowest correlation, and in fact the only one that did not reach statistical significance. This suggests that although line managers appreciate the strategic activities of HR, they still heavily emphasize HR's ability to deliver its services, particularly those related to recruiting and developing talent, when they think about HR effectiveness. For HR, it suggests that the strategic activities closely tied to the strategy process are more strongly emphasized in perceptions of HR effectiveness.

The extent to which the HR function has a highly developed HR strategy and role in driving strategic change is strongly related to HR executives' ratings of HR effectiveness. Table 14.3 shows that all the relationships between the HR strategy items and effectiveness are statistically significant in both the 2004 and 2007 data. The weakest relationship in 2004 concerned analytics support for business decision making. In 2007, however, this correlation is the highest. This suggests an increasing realization of the value of a decision-science paradigm for HR, in which the mandate is extended to the quality of decision support, not just services and compliance.

According to the results in both Table 14.2 and Table 14.3, HR is seen as most effective when it focuses on both contributing to business strategy and developing a robust human capital and functional strategy. Perhaps the best overall conclusion is that HR is most effective when it plays a major role in business strategy development and implementation as well as having a well-developed HR strategy.

Table 14.3. Relationship of HR strategy to HR effectiveness		
	HR Effectiveness[1]	
HR Strategy Activities	**2004**	**2007**
Data-based talent strategy	.49***	**.38***
Partner with line in developing business strategy	.45***	**.59***
A human capital strategy that is integrated with business strategy	.46***	**.53***
Provides analytic support for business decision making	.34*	**.68***
Provides HR data to support change management	.42**	**.62***
HR drives change management	.42**	**.60***
Makes rigorous data-based decisions about human capital management	.46***	**.62***

[1] Based on total score for all thirteen effectiveness items as rated by HR executives.
Significance level: [t] $p \leq .10$; * $p \leq .05$; ** $p \leq .01$; *** $p \leq .001$

HR Organization and Activities

The effectiveness of the HR organization is clearly related to certain features of how it is organized. As can be seen in Table 14.4, the results from 2001, 2004, and 2007 are very similar. The use of service teams is strongly related to HR effectiveness, as is the use of information technology. Service teams, enabled by information technology, have shown consistently positive relationships with other aspects of HR's strategic role, so these results reinforce the value of those approaches. It is also notable that the resource efficiency scale is positively correlated with HR effectiveness, indicating that HR organizations can still enhance their effectiveness through attention to their use of scarce resources. As we noted earlier, this means that HR functions should not so much shift away from efficiency to strategy but rather encompass both.

It is somewhat surprising that doing HR talent development for the HR staff is not related to the effectiveness of the HR organization in 2004. There is a somewhat stronger relationship in 2007, a result that is more understandable since HR needs a talented workforce.

It is notable that decentralization is not correlated with HR effectiveness in 2001, 2004, or 2007. Much has been written advocating locating HR centrally for efficiency and control, and similarly strong positions are often taken in favor of decentralizing it for responsiveness and flexibility. Our results with respect to the positive effects of service teams and centralization suggest that HR organizations do need to have a strong corporate center.

The relationship between HR activity changes in the last five to seven years and HR effectiveness is shown in Table 14.5. In 2001, only one item shows a strong relationship, and that is increased attention to compensation and benefits. The results in 2004 show only one strong relationship,

Table 14.4. Relationship of HR organization to HR effectiveness			
	HR Effectiveness[1]		
HR Organization[2]	2001	2004	2007
HR service teams	.35***	.53***	**.39***
Decentralization	.10	.02	**-.04**
Resource efficiency	—	.28*	**.22***
Information technology	—	.59***	**.35***
HR talent development	—	-.01	**.20[t]**

[1] Based on total score for all thirteen effectiveness items as rated by HR executives.

[2] See Table 6.1 for items in scales.

Significance level: $^t p \leq .10$; $^* p \leq .05$; $^{**} p \leq .01$; $^{***} p \leq .001$

Table 14.5. Relationship of HR activities changes to HR effectiveness			
	HR Effectiveness[1]		
HR Activities[2]	2001	2004	2007
Organization and planning	.18[t]	.29*	**.37***
Compensation and benefits	.28**	−.08	**.05**
Employee development	.11	.20	**.23***
Recruitment and selection	.07	.13	**.06**
Metrics	—	.16	**.20***
HR information systems	.08	−.10	**−.07**
Union relations	−.06	.16	**−.15**

[1] Based on total score for all thirteen effectiveness items as rated by HR executives.

[2] See Table 7.1 for items in scales.

Significance level: [t] $p \leq .10$; * $p \leq .05$; ** $p \leq .01$; *** $p \leq .001$

for organization and planning. In 2007, HR effectiveness is still strongly related to increasing time on planning and design, but in addition we see significant relationships with increasing the time spent on employee development and metrics.

Notice that Table 14.5 deals not with the absolute amount of time or the effectiveness of these activities, but with the change in time spent. Table 14.2 showed that the amount of time spent on recruiting and developing talent was related to HR effectiveness. Table 14.5 shows that increasing the time spent on recruitment is not significantly related, but increasing the time spent on development is. This might mean that efforts devoted to recruitment were already at appropriate levels, and those activities are related to effectiveness, but that in 2007 employee development was more of an emerging area, in which increased time makes a significant difference in effectiveness.

From 2004 to 2007, the relationship of increased attention to metrics with effectiveness became stronger, and indeed reached a significant level in 2007. As we have seen, the effectiveness of HR measurement and analytics is related to HR's strategic role as well. Again, this may suggest that metrics have now reached the point at which increased attention makes a significant difference in the impact of the HR function, perhaps because of an increasing technical capability to develop effective HRISs and meaningful metrics that tie closely to functional and organizational success.

Outsourcing

Table 14.6, which focuses on the relationship between outsourcing and HR effectiveness, shows no statistically significant relationships ($p \leq .05$) in 2004 or in 2007. The general trend is toward low positive relationships

Table 14.6. Relationship of outsourcing to HR effectiveness		
	HR Effectiveness[1]	
Type of Outsourcing	**2004**	**2007**
Overall outsourcing	.19	**−.05**
Planning	−.25[t]	**−.19[t]**
Organization design and development	−.09	**−.06**
Training	.13	**.00**
HRIS and record keeping	.23[t]	**−.01**
Staffing and career development	.24[t]	**.01**
Metrics	.17	**.05**
Compensation	.06	**−.04**
Benefits	.00	**−.10**
Legal affairs	.24[t]	**−.03**
Employee assistance	.19	**−.12**
Competency/talent assessment	.26[t]	**.13**
Union relations	−.15	**.02**

[1] Based on total score for all thirteen effectiveness items as rated by HR executives.

Significance level: [t] $p \leq .10$; * $p \leq .05$; ** $p \leq .01$; *** $p \leq .001$

in 2004 and low negative relationships in 2007. The degree to which individual activities are outsourced clearly is not a significant predictor or cause of HR effectiveness.

It is interesting to note that there is a negative correlation between outsourcing HR planning activities and HR effectiveness in both 2004 and 2007. This is the only item that reached marginal significance ($p \leq .10$) in both years, and it is negative in both. Our data show (see Table 8.1) that fewer than 10 percent of companies outsource planning, and then only partially. Thus it is unusual for organizations to do this, so the finding may reflect the pattern that HR planning is outsourced only as an extreme measure, perhaps because HR planning is not being delivered effectively, by a generally ineffective HR group. Thus ineffective HR functions may find that they are vulnerable to having HR planning outsourced. It is also possible, but less likely, that the causation goes the other way, and that organizations that outsource planning make their HR organizations less effective.

Information Technology

The results from 2001 show a strong positive relationship between IT use and HR effectiveness. This relationship was present in 2004, but not statistically significant. It again reached significance in 2007. As can be seen in Table 14.7, those organizations with completely integrated systems tend to be rated as the most effective. Also, the greater the presence of IT and the more HR processes that are IT-based, the greater the effectiveness. This finding is consistent with the finding (see Chapter 11) that those HR functions which use information technology for the most HR processes tend to be perceived as the most effective.

Table 14.8 provides more detail concerning the relationship between information technology and HR effectiveness. In this table, we examine not the use of IT but the outcomes of the HRIS, as they relate to HR effectiveness. Here our results show strong positive correlations in both 2004 and 2007. In 2004 efficiency generated the highest correlation, while in 2007 the correlations are very similar (though somewhat lower) across all the outcomes. This suggests that there may be a trend toward broader expectations of HRIS contributions than efficiency through cost-cutting.

Table 14.7. Relationship of information system use to HR effectiveness			
	Mean HR Effectiveness[1]		
Information System	2001*	2004	2007*
Completely integrated HR IT system	6.6	7.8	**7.5**
Most processes are IT-based but not fully integrated	6.5	7.0	**6.6**
Some HR processes are IT-based	6.0	6.5	**6.1**
Little IT present in the HR function	4.6	6.5	**5.6**
No IT present	5.6	No respondents	**4.7**

Response scale: 1 = Not meeting needs, 10 = All needs met
[1] Based on total score for all thirteen effectiveness items as rated by HR executives.
*Significant difference in HR effectiveness ($p \leq .05$) among information system use levels.

Table 14.8. Relationship of HRIS outcomes to HR effectiveness		
	HR Effectiveness[1]	
HRIS Outcomes[2]	2004	2007
Overall (All Items)	.43***	**.36***
Employee satisfaction	.52***	**.36***
Efficiency	.64***	**.32**
Business effectiveness	.48***	**.34***
Improve human capital decisions of managers outside HR	—	**.30**
Effective	—	**.36***

[1] Based on total score for all thirteen effectiveness items as rated by HR executives.
[2] See Table 11.3 for items in scales.
Significance level: [t] $p \leq .10$; * $p \leq .05$; ** $p \leq .01$; *** $p \leq .001$

It is also notable that the new 2007 item reflecting the HRIS's effectiveness in improving human capital decisions among those outside HR shows a relationship with HR effectiveness similar to the other items. This suggests that today HRISs contribute to HR effectiveness across a wide spectrum of outcomes, ranging from efficiency to effectiveness and impact.

The use of HR metrics and analytics is strongly related to HR effectiveness. As can be seen in Table 14.9, greater use of HR metrics is associated with greater HR effectiveness in efficiency, effectiveness, and impact. This again supports the proposition that, like other disciplines such as finance and marketing, attention to all three areas is important, and measures of one cannot substitute for others.

As in 2004, the only use that does not show a strong significant relationship to effectiveness is benchmarking analytics and measures against data from outside organizations. This may be because benchmarking has become such a common practice that it offers no unique value. The

Table 14.9. Relationship of HR metrics and analytics use to HR effectiveness		
	HR Effectiveness[1]	
Use of Metrics and Analytics	**2004**	**2007**
Efficiency		
Measure the financial efficiency of HR operations (e.g., cost-per-hire, time-to-fill, training costs)?	.51***	**.37***
Collect metrics that measure the cost of providing HR programs and processes?	.44***	**.51***
Benchmark analytics and measures against data from outside organizations (Saratoga, Mercer, Hewitt, etc.)?	.16	**.18**[t]
Effectiveness		
Use HR dashboards or scorecards? *(2004) Use dashboards or scorecards to evaluate HR's performance?*	.39**	**.32***
Measure the specific effects of HR programs (such as learning from training, motivation from rewards, validity of tests, etc.)?	—	**.33***
Have the capability to conduct cost-benefit analyses (also called utility analyses) of HR programs?	.51***	**.24***
Impact		
Measure the business impact of HR programs and processes? *(2004) Collect metrics that measure the business impact of HR programs and processes?*	.41**	**.32***
Measure the quality of the talent decisions made by non-HR leaders?	—	**.27***
Measure the business impact of high versus low performance in jobs?	—	**.23***
[1] Based on total score for all thirteen effectiveness items as rated by HR executives. Significance level: [t] $p \le .10$; * $p \le .05$; ** $p \le .01$; *** $p \le .001$		

other notable difference between 2007 and 2004 is that the capability to conduct cost-benefit analysis of HR programs is more strongly related to HR effectiveness in 2004 than in 2007. This may be because the ability to do such analyses is more common, or that cost-benefit analysis is now seen more as one of many ways to contribute to HR effectiveness.

Table 14.10 examines the relationship between the effectiveness of metrics and analytics and overall HR effectiveness. It shows that the effectiveness of HR is strongly related to the effectiveness of an organization's HR metrics and analytics activities. As can be seen in Table 14.10, all of the items concerned with metrics and analytics effectiveness are strongly related to HR effectiveness, including strategic and HR functional elements. This is also true for all the elements of the LAMP framework.

Somewhat surprisingly, there is little difference in the size of the correlations in Table 14.10. Slightly higher correlations exist for metrics having

Table 14.10. Relationship of HR metrics and analytics effectiveness to HR effectiveness		
	HR Effectiveness[1]	
Metrics and Analytics Effectiveness	2004	2007
Strategy Contributions		
Supporting organizational change efforts	.44***	**.56***
Contributing to decisions about business strategy and human capital management	.52***	**.54***
Assessing and improving the human capital strategy of the company	.52***	**.59***
Identifying where talent has the greatest potential for strategic impact	.47***	**.44***
Making decisions and recommendations that reflect your company's competitive situation	.43***	**.52***
Connecting human capital practices to organizational performance	.41**	**.55***
Assessing the feasibility of new business strategies	.45***	**.53***
HR Functional and Operational Contributions		
Assessing and improving the HR department operations	.60***	.61***
Evaluating the effectiveness of most HR programs and practices	.54***	**.52***
Assessing HR programs before they are implemented—not just after they are operational	.48***	**.47***
Pinpointing HR programs that should be discontinued	.54***	**.51***
Logic, Analysis, Measurement, and Process (LAMP)		
Using logical principles that clearly connect talent to organization success	—	**.54***
Using advanced data analysis and statistics	—	**.51***
Providing high-quality (complete, timely, accessible) talent measurements	—	**.50***
Motivating users to take appropriate action	—	**.53***
[1] Based on total score for all thirteen effectiveness items as rated by HR executives. Significance level: $^t p \le .10$; $* p \le .05$; $** p \le .01$; $*** p \le .001$		

to do with the HR functional and operational contributions, as in 2004, but all of the activities are significantly related to the effectiveness of the HR function. This suggests that having effective HR analytics and metrics in almost any area is a way to improve the effectiveness of the HR function—possibly because it helps to make the HR organization more strategic, and that, in turn, makes it more effective. It is also possible that even for metrics that are not used directly to make strategic decisions (such as those focusing on HR department operations), their existence signals rigor and effectiveness. At this point in the evolution of the HR profession, demonstrating effective use of metrics and analytics in virtually any HR area may be a significant contributor to HR effectiveness.

The best conclusion concerning the use of metrics and analytics is that their use is clearly tied to the effectiveness of the HR function and that the HR function needs to make increasing use of them. It is particularly important that HR develop greater effectiveness in metrics and analytics, considering the relatively low effectiveness ratings the metrics analytics items received from HR executives (see Table 9.1). The typical response was "somewhat effective" to all of these items. Clearly, there is room for improvement.

Decision Science

The sophistication of managers' decision science about human capital is clearly and strongly related to HR effectiveness, as was the case in 2004. As can be seen in Table 14.11, most of the decision-science items are highly correlated at approximately equal levels with effectiveness both for HR executives and line managers.

The item reflecting HR adding value through compliance is only marginally significant among the HR executives, but is strongly significant for managers (this item is also the only one that is not significantly correlated with HR effectiveness among the HR executives). Managers also rated this item significantly higher in effectiveness than did HR executives (see Table 5.1). Perhaps compliance is seen as passé among HR executives, but line leaders perceive significant value in improving it.

The opposite pattern is seen in the traditional business skill areas. For managers, HR effectiveness is not significantly related to their ratings of the extent to which business leaders use sound principles in decisions about business strategy, finance, or technology. Only business leaders' skills in marketing principles are significantly related to HR effectiveness.

For HR executives, all of the business skill areas are significantly related to their perceptions of HR effectiveness. Perhaps HR executives, working hard to connect to business decisions, vividly see the difficulty of being effective if business decisions are not well grounded and sophisticated.

Table 14.11. Relationship of decision-science sophistication to HR effectiveness

Decision Making	Correlation with HR Effectiveness			
	2004		2007	
	HR Executives[1]	Managers[2]	HR Executives[1]	Managers[2]
We excel at competing for and with talent where it matters most to our strategic success.	—	—	.45***	.48**
Business leaders' decisions that depend on or affect human capital (e.g., layoffs, rewards, etc.) are as rigorous, logical, and strategically relevant as their decisions about resources such as money, technology, and customers.	.45***	.65***	.53***	.61***
Business leaders understand and use sound principles when making decisions about:				
1. Motivation	.44***	.38**	.51***	.51***
2. Development and learning	.39**	.44***	.54***	.53***
3. Labor markets	.48***	.47***	.46***	.44**
4. Culture	.46***	.63***	.57***	.58***
5. Organization design	.61***	.72***	.54***	.68***
6. Business strategy	.49***	.50***	.47***	.12
7. Finance	—	—	.22*	–.09
8. Marketing	—	—	.36***	.38*
9. Technology	—	—	.45***	.22
HR leaders identify unique strategy insights by connecting human capital issues to business strategy.	.62***	.69***	.65***	.73***
HR leaders have a good understanding about where and why human capital makes the biggest difference in their business.	.53***	.61***	.62***	.68***
Business leaders have a good understanding about where and why human capital makes the biggest difference in their business.	.48***	.51***	.60***	.58***
HR systems educate business leaders about their talent decisions.	—	—	.45***	.69***
HR adds value by ensuring compliance with rules, laws, and guidelines.	—	—	.18t	.46**
HR adds value by delivering high-quality professional practices and services.	—	—	.60***	.68***
HR adds value by improving talent decisions inside and outside the HR function	—	—	.57***	.75***

Response Scale: 1 = Little or no extent; 2 = Some extent; 3 = Moderate extent; 4 = Great extent; 5 = Very great extent

[1] Based on total score for all thirteen effectiveness items as rated by HR executives.

[2] Based on total score for all thirteen effectiveness items as rated by managers.

Significance level: t p ≤ .10; * p ≤ .05; ** p ≤ .01; *** p ≤ .001

On the other hand, managers may still see HR as separate from other business disciplines.

The pattern of correlations in Table 14.11 is interesting. In the cases of both HR executives and managers, the highest correlations are with HR providing unique strategy insights, the talent segmentation behaviors of both HR and business leaders, and HR delivering high-quality practices. In addition, managers show strong associations with business leaders' talent decisions having similar rigor to other resources, HR systems that educate business leaders about their talent decisions, and HR's value in improving talent decisions inside and outside the HR function. Managers also associate business leaders' use of sound principles in organization design somewhat more with HR effectiveness than with the other human capital decisions.

In general, business leaders may associate HR's ability to improve their talent decisions, and inform them of their quality, as somewhat more strongly associated with effective HR than HR leaders do. This may represent an opportunity for HR to advance its effectiveness by putting a greater emphasis on improving decision quality, not just within the HR function but among those outside it.

As in 2004, our results generally suggest that the decision skills of business leaders outside of HR are highly related to HR effectiveness. This result suggests that not only does it take the right HR design, staffing, and practices for HR to be effective, it also takes well-prepared "clients" (business executives).

Skill Satisfaction

Table 14.12 shows the relationships between HR effectiveness and the satisfaction of HR executives and managers with the skills of HR. In both 2004 and 2007, there are strong correlations for all the skills; the lowest (but still statistically significant) is for managing outsourcing. This relationship, particularly in the case of HR executives, is not as strong as for the other types of skills. This may reflect the fact that in many companies there is little or no outsourcing, so the skill is not relevant. The strong relationship for the other skills once again confirms the importance of HR professionals having skills beyond just HR technical skills.

Table 14.12. Relationship of HR skill satisfaction to HR effectiveness				
	HR Effectiveness			
	2004		**2007**	
HR Skills[3]	**HR Executives[1]**	**Managers[2]**	**HR Executives[1]**	**Managers[2]**
HR technical skills	.59***	.66***	**.55***	**.68***
Interpersonal dynamics	.63***	.79***	**.67***	**.70***
Business partner skills	.65***	.80***	**.79***	**.78***
Metrics skills	.58***	.57***	**.68***	**.65***
Managing outsourcing	.33*	.61***	**.41***	**.57***

[1] Based on total score for all thirteen effectiveness items as rated by HR executives.
[2] Based on total score for all thirteen effectiveness items as rated by managers.
[3] See Table 12.3. for items in scales.
Significance level: [t] $p \le .10$; * $p \le .05$; ** $p \le .01$; *** $p \le .001$

Particularly strong relationships exist for interpersonal dynamics and business partner skills, as well as metrics. As we noted earlier, these skills are rated only moderately present and effective by both HR executives and managers, so these results reinforce the conclusion that there remains a significant opportunity for enhanced HR effectiveness through skill-building within and beyond HR technical skills.

Importance of HR Practices and Activities

To determine the relative importance of the many practices, structures, and skills that are associated with HR effectiveness, a final analysis was performed. A regression analysis was run using key items from Tables 14.1 to 14.12. The following items (in the order of predictive power) were the best predictors of HR effectiveness.

1. Satisfaction with business partner skills

2. Provision of analytics support for business decision making

3. An HRIS that improves HR operations

4. Increased activity in organization design and development

Once again, our data suggest that HR needs to perform well in its administrative functions, as well as be a business partner and a strategic partner. In terms of relative importance, the data suggest that business and strategy are the most important.

Conclusion

Our results show a number of strong relationships between the effectiveness of the HR function and the way it is organized, managed, and staffed. Among the most important findings are the following:

- The amount of time spent on maintaining records is negatively related to effectiveness, while time spent on being a strategic partner is positively related.

- Strategic activities such as designing an organization's criteria for strategic success and choosing strategy options are strongly related to HR effectiveness.

- Using information technology and service teams as delivery mechanisms for HR services is strongly related to HR effectiveness.

- Increased focus on organization design and development is related to HR effectiveness.

- Having a completely integrated HRIS system leads to the highest level of HR effectiveness.

- The effectiveness of the HRIS system is strongly related to the overall effectiveness of the HR organization.

- Having a wide array of effective HR metrics and analytics is strongly related to HR effectiveness.

- The effectiveness of the HR metrics system is strongly related to HR effectiveness.

- The decision-science sophistication of both business leaders and HR leaders is strongly related to the effectiveness of the HR function.

- There is a clear relationship between the skills of HR managers and the effectiveness of the HR function.

Overall, the findings tell an important story. HR effectiveness is associated with a wide array of HR activities, structures, systems, and skills that are within the control of HR. HR can do a lot to make itself more effective. It needs to be sure its administrative processes work well, but its best opportunities for improvement appear to be in the business partner role and the strategic partner role.

CHAPTER 15

HR Excellence

There is no question that the HR function in most organizations needs to look very different than it did ten to fifteen years ago. Further, there is widespread agreement concerning a number of broad themes: it needs to be more strategic, it needs to be more of a business partner, it needs to offer high-quality administrative services, and it needs to be an expert in human capital management. But is the HR function changing? If it is, what is the nature of that change?

Our study provides unique data to answer questions about whether and how HR is changing. Other studies have asked about the importance of HR taking new directions, adding new skills, and offering new services, and they have asked HR managers to report on the amount and kind of change they think has occurred. Our study is the only one that has examined change by measuring the activities of HR functions over two decades.

Reports of change are almost always less valid than are comparisons among data collected at two or more points in time. The former are influenced by memory and other factors. The problem with reports of change is demonstrated in our study by the responses to our question concerning how time is spent.

HR executives responding to each of our five surveys report that there has been a significant shift in the way HR time is being spent. However, when we examine changes in activity levels using reports of current practice from different time periods, the percentages have not shifted. This is much better evidence about the kind and amount of change that has happened than are reports of whether change has occurred.

What Has and Hasn't Changed

Our analysis of the results of our 1995, 1998, 2001, 2004, and 2007 surveys establishes that a number of significant changes have occurred in how HR functions are organized and how they deliver services. The most significant changes involve the way the HR function is organized, where HR activities and information are located, and HR's role in employee advocacy and shaping a labor market strategy. These changes may well set the stage for creating a greater strategic partnership for HR, but they are largely focused on how the HR function itself is organized and managed, and how it defines its relationships with its clients. The most important changes are the following:

- HR is more likely to use service teams to support and service business units.

- HR is more likely to have corporate centers of excellence.

- Companies are more likely to have similar HR practices in different business units.

- HR is paying increased attention to recruitment and selection as well as organization design and development.

- The use of outsourcing for a number of HR activities has increased.

- More companies have integrated HRISs that can perform a number of HR activities.

- Employees and managers are increasingly making use of HRISs that provide job information and performance management capabilities.

- There is greater satisfaction with the interpersonal dynamics and business-understanding skills of HR professionals.

- HR is increasingly effective in helping shape a viable employment relationship for the future, providing HR services, operating centers of excellence, and being an employee advocate.

In comparing the 1995 and 1998 results to the 2007 results, it is clear that a number of things have not changed very much, if at all. Many of these elements reflect HR's role in shaping strategy and building important HR skills. Among them are the following:

- The amount of time spent on various human resource activities

- HR executives' belief that HR is spending more time being a strategic partner

- The extent to which HR is a full partner in shaping business strategy

- The failure to rotate individuals into, out of, and within HR

- The desire of HR executives to have HR be a business and strategic partner

- The use of shared services

- The problems that occur with outsourcing

- The use of outsourcing for organization development, employee assistance, and HR planning

- The percentage of HR professionals who have the skills they need to be effective

- Most of the business partner skills of the HR professionals

- The importance of HR services

- The characteristics of an effective HR function

Overall, when we compare our data from 1995, 1998, 2001, 2004, and 2007, we see that more things have stayed the same than have changed. Although many of the changes we found are significant and important, the amount of change is surprisingly small. Frankly, given the tremendous amount of attention that has been given to the importance of HR becoming a business and strategic partner, and adding value in new ways, we expected much more change. In fact, we have expected more change than we have seen in every survey since the study began. This "stubborn traditionalism" (Boudreau and Ramstad 2007) is also apparent in continuing articles about frustration among organization leaders with HR's unfulfilled potential.

While much about HR's role in corporations has remained the same, the amount of change that is going on around it appears to have increased dramatically (O'Toole and Lawler 2006). This raises a critical question: Are there particular organizational conditions that are associated with HR being more of a business and strategic partner? The answer should help us understand what it takes to change HR organizations.

Strategic Focuses

Our study found a strong relationship between what is happening in the HR function and an organization's strategic focuses. In particular, the degree to which organizations had knowledge and organizational performance strategies is related to how much the HR function fits the vision of HR as a business and strategic partner. To a lesser extent, the same was true of companies with strategies focusing on quality and speed but, somewhat to our surprise, not growth. Companies that reported HR was a full partner, or had an input role to business strategy, have a greater emphasis on knowledge- and information-based strategies. Generally speaking, it appears that an emphasis on knowledge, information, and human capital creates a much more favorable situation for the HR function because it places a premium on acquiring, developing, deploying, and retaining talent.

One interesting theme in our results is the association of an emphasis on knowledge and information with the use and the effectiveness of HRISs. This is especially true with respect to their providing knowledge and management tools. An emphasis on HRISs is compatible with current ideas about knowledge management that stress IT as a powerful tool for making knowledge available throughout an organization (Davenport and Prusak 1998). Knowledge can be embedded in tools that extend the knowledge workers' capabilities (Leonard-Barton 1995), including not only the tools that are offered to employees and managers in general but also the tools that are used by HR.

A knowledge focus is also associated with the more interpersonal aspects of HR, such as the use of service teams and the importance of interpersonal dynamics skills. This fits with the proposition that IT is insufficient for delivering knowledge, because the application of knowledge to solve complex and uncertain problems often requires people with different knowledge bases to work together (Mohrman, Finegold, and Klein 2002). Strategies and initiatives that focus on organizational performance capabilities relate to many of the same features of the HR organization as the knowledge emphasis.

Overall, our results clearly show that the various strategy focuses relate differently to the way the HR function operates and to its success as a business partner. When there is a focus on knowledge and organizational performance and, to a lesser extent, quality- and information-based strategies, HR performs more high-valued-added activities, and the HR function is more positively regarded. The same is not consistently true of the other strategy focuses.

These results raise the question of the direction of causality. One possibility is that an organization's strategy causes HR to take on a particular role. The alternative is that a more strategic HR role causes organizations to attempt or adopt strategies that rely more on knowledge and talent quality. Our guess is that the most common causal direction is from strategy to the nature of HR, not the reverse. One implication of this is that how an HR organization operates in a company may be largely determined by the company's business strategy, which in turn cannot be greatly influenced by HR. Perhaps HR is more the victim than the bad guy in cases in which it is not a business or strategic partner. Certainly, more than one of the senior HR leaders we work with has said that it is easier to find an organization that understands and supports strategic HR than to try to change an organization that does not.

Management Approach

We considered four management approaches, and only one had a strong and consistent relationship with the nature of the HR function in organizations. The high-involvement approach was associated with HR being more involved in business strategy activities and employee development, and in working with the board. This is not surprising. The high-involvement approach, perhaps more than others, requires a clear focus on human capital and an organization that understands how talent and organization design decisions affect strategic success.

As with the results for different strategic focuses, there is the question of what comes first—the high-involvement approach or the HR function that is a stronger business and strategic partner. As with the strategic focuses, our best guess is that it is more often the high-involvement approach that leads to the strong HR role, but there are probably organizations where HR has had a major influence on the organization adopting the high-involvement approach.

HR as a Strategic Partner

The data concerning what determines the effectiveness of the HR organization are clearly consistent with the argument that HR can and should be more of a strategic partner. Yet the data also are consistent with the reality that HR is not a strategic partner in most organizations. HR appears to have some influence when it comes to how staffing relates to strategy and in influencing organizational structure and its relationship to implementing strategy. Still, our results suggest HR plays a less prominent role when it comes to the development of strategy, consideration of strategic options, and other strategy areas, including acquisitions and mergers.

Several factors were significantly associated with a stronger strategic role for HR, including

- The use of information technology
- Focusing on HR talent development
- Using HR service teams
- HR activities focused on organization design, organization development, employee development, and metrics
- Using computer systems for training and development
- Having an effective HRIS
- Having effective HR metrics and analytics
- Having business leaders who make rigorous, logical human capital decisions
- Having an HR staff with technical, organizational dynamics; business partner and metrics skills
- Having an HR function that effectively provides services, fulfills its corporate roles, and is effective in supporting business strategy

In general, the model developed by Lawler and Mohrman (2003b), based on our 2001 survey, is supported by the results of the 2007 survey. An updated version of it is presented in Exhibit 15.1. Overall, being a strategic partner demands that high levels of business knowledge and skill be present in HR, that HRISs have the right metrics and analytics, and that organization designs and practices link HR managers to business units. Last but not to be overlooked is the need for effective and efficient delivery of HR services.

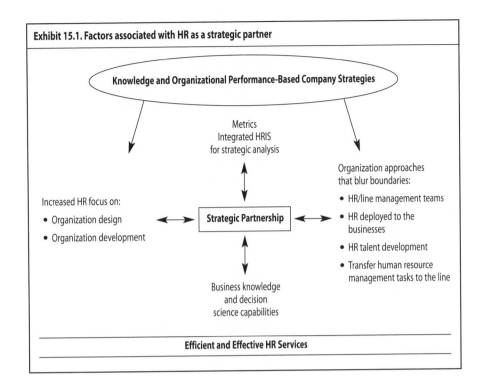

Exhibit 15.1. Factors associated with HR as a strategic partner

Knowledge and Organizational Performance-Based Company Strategies

Metrics
Integrated HRIS
for strategic analysis

Organization approaches
that blur boundaries:

- HR/line management teams
- HR deployed to the businesses
- HR talent development
- Transfer human resource management tasks to the line

Increased HR focus on:

- Organization design
- Organization development

Strategic Partnership

Business knowledge
and decision
science capabilities

Efficient and Effective HR Services

HR Effectiveness

The factors leading to HR effectiveness are a combination of approaches that promote efficiency in routine transactional processing and allow HR professionals to focus on expanding their knowledge base, providing expertise, and partnering with others. In Chapter 14 we provided a long list of practices that are associated with effectiveness; the list provides an actionable agenda for most HR functions. It is also marked by another characteristic: most of the practices are not widely used, and show little increase in use from 1995 to 2007. This strongly suggests that one of the reasons why HR is not increasing in effectiveness is that it has not done the things it needs to do in order to be perceived as more effective.

Obstacles to Change

Why hasn't HR changed more? There are a number of plausible explanations. One is that HR executives simply don't feel HR needs to change. On the basis of the results of our surveys, we can say this isn't true. In all our surveys, HR executives have said they plan to change and have said that it is important that they act as a strategic partner. Of course, they may just be saying what is "professionally correct" and giving lip service to the idea of being a strategic partner, but we don't think this is the case. We think they do want HR to change.

A second reason for the failure of HR to change is that in most organizations there is no great demand for HR to change. The existing role and activities of HR are well institutionalized in a kind of codependency relationship. The individuals in the HR function are comfortable in their current role and in delivering services in a traditional mode; at the same time the recipients of these services are happy to have an administrative function that removes what they see as onerous HR responsibilities from them. This situation leads to an institutionalized devaluation of the HR function because of its low level of contribution to the business, and to an unwillingness to let it change because it serves many in the organization well enough as it is. However, our results showing an increase in the use of centralized HR services, and the movement of HR activities into the hands of employees and their managers, may challenge traditional notions of highly attentive and personal HR service.

The managers outside of HR that we surveyed in 2004 and 2007 acknowledge the importance of HR being a strategic partner, but they seem to focus on HR contributing to strategy through good talent management. Ironically, it is possible that the "war for talent" may be operating against the upgrading of the HR function. It may focus a disproportionate amount of professional HR time on delivering services related to recruiting, orienting, developing, and retaining employees, leaving HR little time and few resources to spend on upgrading its competencies and systems in other areas and being a strategic partner. HR time and attention may be sidetracked by bidding wars for talented employees and by the need to generate and administer reward systems that are constantly being challenged to provide mass customization for scarce talent.

Recruiting, developing, and retaining a highly mobile and competitive workforce can often impose very high demands on process-related time and energy that can lock HR professionals into activity patterns that are difficult to change. Certainly, a common refrain from HR leaders is that they rarely have time to think about bigger-picture issues, or to develop in areas beyond their specific functional responsibilities. We found that the attention being paid to almost all HR activities has increased, suggesting that even though there is a consensus that some HR activities add greater value, HR functions are still required to spend more time on activities that they know to be low in strategic value.

The skills of the HR function offer an additional explanation for the limited change in the HR function. Just how difficult it is to change the HR function becomes apparent when we look at the kinds of skills that members of the HR function must have in order to be rated highly and to play the strategic and business partner roles.

HR professionals need a broad range of skills, ranging from relatively routine administrative processing skills to organizational dynamics and business partner skills. Although business partner and organizational dynamics skills are most highly related to effectiveness, our results suggest that the HR function cannot be ineffective in core administrative functions. Interestingly, HR does not score very highly in administrative skills, especially with respect to managing contractors and managing HRISs. These are relatively new competencies that have become very important with the growing importance of HRISs and outsourcing.

Business and strategic partnering effectiveness requires knowledge and skills in such areas as change management, strategic planning, and organization design. It also requires a decision science for human capital that provides logical and unique strategic insights by using human capital principles. These areas involve complex judgments, and HR professionals have traditionally had little experience with them. Such expertise is both hard to acquire and in short supply. Becoming expert in business partnering demands the acquisition of not only explicit knowledge but also tacit knowledge that comes from experience. Applying this expertise demands the ability to influence line management and to be part of effective teaming relationships with others who carry deep knowledge about the business and the market (Mohrman, Finegold, and Klein 2002).

The results of our study show that although HR professionals are seen as having increased some of their interpersonal dynamics skills and their business-understanding skills since 1995, they are still perceived to fall short in most business partner skills and in metrics analytical skills as well. HR leaders also often lack requisite cross-functional experience. Understanding the business is just a ticket to get to the table. Expertise in other strategy areas is required to add value once at the table. Thus HR is in a bit of a catch-22. It must get to the table and gain experience in order to gain the knowledge and skills it needs to get there!

Conclusion

HR wants to be a strategic partner. The door is open because of the growing recognition that talent is a key determinant of an organization's effectiveness. But HR cannot seem to get through the door in many organizations, much less get a seat at the table. The good news is that our results consistently show a pattern of HR activities, skills, and relationships that lead to HR effectiveness and a stronger strategic role. Difficult as it may be, the nature of the changes that are required is relatively clear.

CHAPTER 16

*What the Future
of HR Should Be*

What does the future hold for the human resources function? What does HR need to do to become a strategic partner? When we reported on our 1998 results, we said, "Change has just begun. The next decade will probably see dramatic change in the human resource function in most companies. The opportunity exists for human resource management to become a true strategic partner, and to help decide how organizations will be managed, what human resource systems will look like, and how human resource services will be created and delivered."

Our 2007 results suggest that many of the changes we expected and hoped for have not taken place. Yes, there has been some change, but it is not the kind of substantial change that we thought would happen. If anything, we feel more strongly today about the importance of change in the HR organization. Organizations in the United States and the developed world have an ever-higher percentage of their employees doing knowledge work. Human capital is becoming increasingly important as a source of competitive advantage, as is intellectual capital.

Our results show that when organizations focus on developing their competencies, capabilities, and knowledge assets, especially in combination with a strong focus on organizational performance, HR is a much stronger strategic and business partner, and the HR function is markedly different. Thus there is good reason to believe that if organizations increasingly pursue strategic focuses and management approaches that draw on deep and widespread human capital excellence, HR will change. Our belief is that this will be more likely a function of HR responding to organizational changes than HR driving those changes.

How should HR be managed and structured? Should it be a large function, employing approximately one out of every one hundred employees, and organized primarily upon a service-delivery paradigm focused on activities such as compensation, training, and staffing? There is good reason to believe that it should not. HR needs to proceed from a deeper and more fundamental perspective on how it adds sufficient value to justify its cost. This is the way its "customers" are increasingly looking at the HR function. While service delivery at a low cost has been commonly believed to achieve the optimization of value relative to cost, our results suggest that this assumption may be increasingly put to the test. Dimensions such as strategic influence, decision support, organizational agility, and sustainability will increasingly define the HR value proposition, and this means that a simple equation that is based on low-cost service will not be sufficient.

HR as a High-Value Contributor

We pointed out in Chapter 1 that as a business, HR potentially can have three product lines, or roles. The first is to execute the processes and activities required in services such as legal compliance, compensation, staffing, development, and deployment.

The second role is to respond to business plans developed by others, helping business units and general managers realize their business plans. In this role, HR provides advice and services concerning how to develop, design, and install HR practices in areas such as employee relations, talent management, organizational development, and change management, and it connects HR practices with business operations.

The third role is helping to set the strategic direction of the organization. It requires developing and assessing the organization's human capital and creating the organizational capabilities required to support the strategic direction. It also requires shaping strategy by providing a unique perspective through the lenses of talent availability and human behavior. This requires individuals who not only understand business strategy but also understand how it relates to organizational capabilities and core competencies and how they connect to pivotal talent and organization decisions. In this role, HR leaders use their knowledge to help the organization set its strategic direction and develop its business plans, consistent with a talent decision science.

HR Administration

The HR services of an organization are increasingly becoming a commodity that can be delivered in many ways. Historically, they were delivered by an in-house HR function often in a more labor-intensive, less integrated, and more costly manner than the best alternative. This approach is increasingly obsolete. One common replacement is Web-based HR systems based on self-service principles. Three models are emerging as ways to acquire and operate the technology needed to deliver HR services.

The first is to use custom systems designed and operated by the organization. This model is currently being used by information technology companies such as Dell, Cisco, Hewlett-Packard, and Microsoft. Some of these systems are very impressive, and allow individuals, on a self-service basis, to perform a number of important HR tasks and access a great deal of information. However, it is highly unlikely that most companies will ever develop the kind of custom systems that have been developed by technology companies; doing so is simply too expensive and time consuming.

A second model involves acquiring software and systems from outside the organization, using one of two approaches. The first is to buy an integrated Web-based system from a major ERP vendor (for example, Oracle or SAP). The second is to acquire individual HR applications from different software vendors for specific tasks such as compensation administration, staffing, and training. Some very good programs exist, and when combined can produce an effective HR system for companies. However, there is a significant disadvantage associated with choosing a set of best-of-breed software applications. Our results suggest there is great value in integration—the best use of HR data often involves integration across multiple HR processes. Software integration is required, and this can be costly and time consuming. This may lead many organizations to acquire integrated, total HR systems rather than individual solutions. On the other hand, we may see the evolution of a core set of data standards, against which multiple software vendors can develop their applications.

The third model is to use business process outsourcing. A number of major corporations have signed contracts to outsource all or most of the administrative aspects of their human resource management processes. Case studies of four early adopters show some cost savings and quality improvement as well as enabling some movement toward HR becoming more of a strategic partner (Lawler, Ulrich, Fitz-enz, and Madden 2004). Recently, more large firms (such as Unilever and Sun Microsystems) have adopted this approach. The results of our 2007 survey also suggest that this approach is growing and typically is seen as being effective.

We cannot say from our results which model will be dominant in the future, but our findings do suggest what the future of HR information systems should be. Our results suggest that an investment in a high-quality HRIS should increase the HR function's credibility and perceived value added, while decreasing the time the function spends on administrative tasks.

We found some evidence of a substitution effect: providing high-quality systems for administrative processing related not only to perceived administrative effectiveness but to perceived effectiveness in all areas. This may occur because a high-quality HRIS allows the function to spend more time on developing valuable new skills and being a business and strategic partner. Furthermore, by offering knowledge and tools to managers and employees, a high-quality HRIS can provide enhanced decision support that increases their effectiveness in HR and talent management.

At this point, HR executives do not perceive HRISs to be particularly effective. They are given relatively high marks by HR executives on improving HR services and speeding up HR processes but are not rated highly in most other areas. Despite this, we believe they can be a key delivery vehicle for HR services and contribute to an enhanced strategic role for HR. In particular, the value of such systems in conveying HR knowledge and decision frameworks to managers and employees represents an untapped opportunity for improving an organization's talent management.

It is unlikely that any approach to HR administration will be dominant by 2010 when we do our next survey. However, it seems likely that the majority of large firms will have highly developed Web-based HR systems, creating the opportunity to build an HR function that not only is more cost effective but also delivers a superior product. In short, such systems have advanced far enough to offer a better business model than the traditional approach to delivering human resource management services and administration.

Business Partner

But what about the business partner activities of HR? Can and should they be outsourced? Can and should they be put on the Web? There is little doubt that some business partner activities can be greatly facilitated by Web technology, outsourcing, or both.

HRISs can collect, aggregate, and analyze ever-increasing amounts of data about the human resources of an organization, at ever-lower costs and higher speeds. Such data can enhance change management, business plan implementation, and the business operations by making human capital information readily available and by obtaining feedback and suggestions about HR process improvement and effectiveness. It should be pointed out that HRISs are merely enablers; they can enhance but cannot replace human judgment in problem solving and decision making.

As for outsourcing the business partner role, many consultants are very skilled at providing insight about the HR implications of business plans and organizational change. However, our view is that at some point, tailoring HR programs and practices to specific strategies and business plans will always need the contributions of at least some internal HR professionals; they need to provide the services, information, and knowledge that are necessary for HR to be an effective business partner.

Performing the business partner role entails solving problems and making decisions that are value laden, highly uncertain, and context specific; it requires understanding the business, its strategy, the nature of the workforce, and the required competencies. It entails the application of tacit, experience-based knowledge of employee relations as well as knowledge of the HR discipline and the ability to combine HR knowledge with the perspectives of other disciplines such as business management, marketing, information technology, and technology.

The key question here is not whether HR professionals should perform the business partner role, but whether the current cadre of HR professionals is able to perform it. The evidence in our study suggests that the comfort level and effectiveness of human resource professionals is highest with traditional service activities and delivery, but that is not good enough. For HR professionals to be effective business partners, they need to enhance their capabilities in areas such as system design, vendor management, and decision support.

Strategic Partner

Perhaps the most intriguing results are those that have implications for the strategic partner role. As organizations have done more knowledge work and human capital has become more important, there is an increasing need for HR leaders not only to respond to strategies but actually to shape them based on their unique perspective. The rapid rate of change, the need to develop new strategies and to quickly translate them into human resource strategies, and the likelihood that the availability of talent will be a key strategic differentiator have greatly increased the importance of HR being a strategic partner.

The role of strategic partner requires individuals who understand how business strategies and plans connect to talent and organization management. They also need to know how to shape business strategies to fit emerging human capital opportunities and threats. Some of this work can be outsourced to HR strategy consultants; however, we believe there needs to be a strong internal presence of individuals who have good HR knowledge, who can manage consultants, and who can be fully engaged when strategies are formulated. HR's strategic partner role ultimately needs to be led by a senior executive in the organization, not by a consultant.

The importance of the strategic partner role, and the need to fill it with somebody who understands business, may be one reason why almost a quarter of all chief HR executives come from the business rather than from the HR function. In essence, some companies seem to have decided that the HR strategic partner role is too important to be entrusted to someone with exclusively an HR background.

The assumption that someone without HR knowledge is the best person to lead HR is flawed. Just as with other functions such as IT, operations, legal, supply chain, and finance, this role not only requires a strong facility with business and strategy, it requires knowledge of the function. In the case of HR it requires the capacity to understand the principles and practices that underlie labor markets, human behavior at work, and organizational effectiveness. In the same way, knowledge about portfolio theory or customer behavior is a prerequisite to be the chief financial officer or chief marketing officer.

Having data available from an effective HRIS is one of several enablers that can strengthen HR executives' position as strategic partners. HRISs can, for example, help them make significant contributions to strategy formulation, by providing both cost and organizational effectiveness data with respect to human resource practices. They can provide information about how to develop certain key competencies and about the existing levels of organizational effectiveness and organizational capabilities. These are all critical inputs to the strategy planning process. They can codify and teach decision frameworks and principles that enhance strategic decisions. They also can enable HR executives to translate what they know about the existing organization and its capabilities into change programs, thus allowing the organization to develop the necessary capabilities to implement new strategic plans and new directions (Lawler and Worley 2006).

HR Organization Design

An increasingly common feature of HR organizations, particularly in companies with multiple business units, is placing HR executives in each business unit. This business-unit role involves HR contributing to business-unit plans and organizational capabilities. It supports some tailoring of human resource practices to the workforce needs of the business unit.

HR executives in the business units are expected to be liaisons to the corporate HR staff on behalf of their business units. This liaison role is likely to be increasingly important in the future. Instead of locating many of the HR services in the business unit, multidivision corporations are creating shared services units and corporate centers of excellence for the business units to draw on. Or, they are outsourcing HR transactional services and requiring business units to use them. In both approaches the role of the business-unit HR executive is to both translate business strategies into HR responses and coordinate an array of centralized HR services for the business unit.

In essence, the HR organization appears to be becoming a type of front-back organization in which the business-unit HR leader or "generalist" is the front, customer-focused part. The back, in this case, is the vendors, shared services units, and centers of excellence that are available to the business units.

Our results show that the front-back approach to HR function design has increased in popularity since 1994 and that it is an effective design. There is no reason to believe that it will not be the most popular approach in the future. The increasing capability and sophistication of distributed Web-based systems, that we noted earlier, reinforces the value and feasibility of this approach.

Talent Management

Quite possibly the biggest change that needs to occur in HR has to do with talent management—not elsewhere in organizations, but how talent is managed in HR. In many respects talent management in HR is a case of the shoemakers' children lacking shoes. Our results suggest that HR often doesn't have the right talent; all too often it has talent that is inferior to the talent in other key parts of the organization.

HR professionals need to understand and be able to formulate a business model for the HR function and to contribute to the firm's business model. They need to understand business operations and be able to craft human resource management approaches that reflect their organization's competitive situation. They need to understand organization and work design and change management principles and approaches, and be able to play a leadership role when these issues are considered. They need to understand different models of staffing, compensation, and other human resource management practices so that they can effectively implement HR systems that support the business plans of the organization. They need to educate and develop business leaders to make human capital decisions that are as logical, rigorous, and strategic as are their decisions about money, technology, and customers. Finally, they need to identify the pivot points in the business that drive strategic and organizational effectiveness, and then connect human capital decisions to those pivot points.

Admittedly, the skills and knowledge that HR professionals need are not easily acquired. They are only likely to exist in organizations that take HR talent management seriously and have a very integrated approach to talent management. This has important implications for HR's performance and staffing practices at all levels.

At the entry level, HR needs to significantly increase the quality of its hires. Today, few of the best students in the leading business schools pursue HR careers, because of low starting salaries and a perception that HR is not a good place to start a career. As a result, there often is a scarcity of highly talented business-school students with an academic concentration in HR. Organizations therefore need to consider hiring non-HR majors who are very talented and interested in HR. Indeed, the ground may be shifting, as some business-school students have been very articulate about the wisdom of their decision to pursue an HR career (Breitfelder and Dowling 2008). However, at least until it does shift, HR needs to hire non-HR majors.

Once hired, it is important that HR professionals spend time working outside HR. Our data suggest that this doesn't happen very often and that most organizations don't plan on increasing its frequency. This is a problem, because without experience in non-HR jobs, HR professionals miss important opportunities to understand the business, and they miss the chance to build personal credibility by doing a non-HR job well.

It may be even more important to have non-HR managers and professionals rotate into HR than it is for HR professionals to rotate out. At this point, very few U.S. corporations have CEOs or senior executives other than the head of HR who have worked in HR. Increasing the frequency with which senior managers have HR experience has important benefits. First, it can improve their performance when they make human capital decisions and when they work with HR. Second, it makes top organizational talent available to the HR function, and brings to HR the perspective of those non-HR executives regarding HR's value proposition.

Our results show that business leaders are held to higher standards regarding their capability to use sound principles in areas such as finance and marketing, as compared to human capital and talent management. Considering the acknowledged importance of talent to competitiveness, it would seem prudent to give senior leaders deep experience in HR so that they can build their understanding of it.

The value of shared and valid principles about human capital and talent has implications for future HR executives. HR professionals should be trained and should develop and use research-based knowledge about labor markets, human behavior, and organization theory. They need to move beyond just being good to work with and knowledgeable about people and employee relations. They need to know and act on the large amount of research that has been done on talent management, organization design, and a host of other HR issues. Making decisions on instinct or "knowing people" just isn't good enough.

Has the talent level in HR been improving? At least at the senior levels there are some reasons to think it has. More CEOs do recognize the importance of having a talented HR executive and have acted on this recognition. Organizations have been particularly willing to promote women to senior management positions in HR. As a result, many highly talented female business leaders have chosen careers in HR and have become HR executives. This has created a diversity among the senior executives in many corporations that offers significant opportunities for the HR profession to provide a unique perspective, particularly as organizations must consider more diverse employee populations and customers. The downside of this is that many women end up in the HR silo and miss out on opportunities elsewhere in the organization.

Looking Ahead

The opportunity for the human resource function to add value at the strategic level is very great and increasing, but at the present time it is more promise than reality. For promise to become reality, HR executives need to develop new skills and knowledge, and HR needs to be able to execute human resource management and administration activities effectively. Doing the basics well is the platform upon which the HR organization needs to build its role as a strategic partner. Doing so is critical, because it demonstrates the capacity of the HR function to operate effectively as a business, and it potentially can provide the information that enables HR to be an effective strategic partner.

The need for a new business model for HR has been accepted and acknowledged by most HR executives, but the human resource function still appears to be at the very beginning of the changes that are needed in order for it to become a reality. Our study demonstrates that the change process is slower than anticipated, but it has identified a very clear action agenda that can yield an HR function capable of adding more value to the business. We still believe there will be enormous change in the design and operation of human resource functions, but we are not sure it will occur in this decade.

Since we collected our data in late 2007, the world economy has been jolted by a major recession. At this point, it is too early to tell how it has affected the world of HR. It certainly has led to reductions in training budgets and layoffs in HR departments, but this doesn't mean that the role of HR has changed.

In some respects, the recession has served to underline the importance of having a strategic partner HR function. In many companies an unprecedented number of decisions are being made about human capital— Whom to keep? What costs to cut? These are just the kinds of decisions a strategic HR function should be able to provide valuable input to. The recession may serve to highlight the importance of having an effective HR function. Only time will tell if in 2010 when our next survey is done, there will be an increase or decrease in the extent to which HR functions are strategic partners.

We are sure that HR will want to be more of a strategic partner and that it should be. We have said it before and we say it again: the HR function needs to reinvent itself. The old approaches and models are not good enough.

REFERENCES

Becker, B. E., and M. A. Huselid. 1998. High performance work systems and firm performance: A synthesis of research and managerial implications. *Research in Personnel and Human Resources Management* 16:53–101.

Boudreau, J. W., and P. M. Ramstad. 2007. *Beyond HR: The new science of human capital.* Boston: Harvard Business School Press.

Boudreau, J. W., and P. M. Ramstad. 2006. Talentship and human resource management and analysis: From ROI to strategic organizational change. *Human Resource Planning Journal* 29.

Boudreau, J. W., and P. M. Ramstad. 2005a. Talentship and the evolution of human resource management: From "professional practices" to "strategic talent decision science." *Human Resource Planning Journal* 28 (2):17–26.

Boudreau, J. W., and P. M. Ramstad. 2005b. Talentship, talent segmentation, and sustainability: A new HR decision science paradigm for a new strategy definition. In *The future of human resources management,* eds. M. Losey, S. Meisinger, and D. Ulrich. Washington, D.C.: Society for Human Resource Management.

Boudreau, J. W., and P. M. Ramstad. 2005c. Where is your pivotal talent? *Harvard Business Review* 83 (4):23–24.

Boudreau, J. W., and P. M. Ramstad. 2003. Strategic HRM measurement in the 21st century: From justifying HR to strategic talent leadership. In *HRM in the 21st century,* eds. M. Goldsmith, R. P. Gandossy, and M. S. Efron, pp. 79–90. New York: John Wiley & Sons.

Boudreau, J. W., and P. M. Ramstad. 1997. Measuring intellectual capital: Learning from financial history. *Human Resource Management* 36 (3):343–356.

Breitfelder, M. D., and D. W. Dowling. 2008. Why did we ever go into HR? *Harvard Business Review* 86 (7–8):39.

Brockbank, W. 1999. If HR were really strategically proactive: Present and future directions in HR's contribution to competitive advantage. *Human Resource Management* 38:337–52.

Bureau of National Affairs. 2001. *Human resource activities, budgets and staffs.* Washington, D.C.: BNA.

Cascio, W. 2000. *Costing human resources,* 4th ed. Cincinnati: South-Western.

Cascio, W., and J. W. Boudreau. 2008. *Investing in people: Financial impact of human resource initiatives.* Upper Saddle River, N.J.: FT Press.

Csoka, L. S., and B. Hackett. 1998. *Transforming the HR function for global business success.* New York: Conference Board.

Davenport, T. H., and L. Prusak. 1998. *Working knowledge: How organizations manage what they know.* Boston: Harvard Business School Press.

Galbraith, J. R. 2002. *Designing organizations.* San Francisco: Jossey-Bass.

Gates, S. 2008. *Strategic human capital measures.* Research Report R-147-08-WG. New York: Conference Board.

Gates, S. 2004. *Measuring more than efficiency.* Research Report R-1356-04-RR. New York: Conference Board.

Gubman, E. 2004. HR strategy and planning: From birth to business results. *Human Resource Planning* 27 (1): 13–23.

Guthridge, M., A. B. Komm, and E. Lawson. 2008. Making talent a strategic priority. *McKinsey Quarterly* 1: 49–59.

Huselid, M. A., B. E. Becker, and R. W. Beatty. 2005. *The workforce scorecard.* Boston: Harvard Business School Press.

Lawler, E. E. 2008. *Talent: Making people your competitive advantage.* San Francisco: Jossey-Bass.

Lawler, E. E. 2003. *Treat people right! How organizations and individuals can propel each other into a virtuous spiral of success.* San Francisco: Jossey-Bass.

Lawler, E. E. (1995). Strategic human resources management: An idea whose time has come. In *Managing human resources in the 1990s and beyond: Is the workplace being transformed?* eds. B. Downie and M. L. Coates, pp. 46–70. Kingston, Canada: IRC Press.

Lawler, E. E., J. W. Boudreau, and S. A. Mohrman. 2006. *Achieving strategic excellence: An assessment of human resource organizations.* Stanford, Calif.: Stanford University Press.

Lawler, E. E., A. Levenson, and J. W. Boudreau. 2004. HR metrics and analytics—uses and impacts. *Human Resource Planning Journal* 27 (4):27–35.

Lawler, E. E., and S. A. Mohrman. 2003a. *Creating a strategic human resources organization: An assessment of trends and new directions.* Stanford, CA: Stanford University Press.

Lawler, E. E., and S. A. Mohrman. 2003b. HR as a strategic partner: What does it take to make it happen? *Human Resource Planning* 26 (5):15.

Lawler, E. E., and S. A. Mohrman. 2000. *Creating a strategic human resources organization.* Los Angeles: Center for Effective Organizations.

Lawler, E. E., S. A. Mohrman, and G. S. Benson. 2001. *Organizing for high performance: The CEO report on employee involvement, TQM, reengineering, and knowledge management in Fortune 1000 companies.* San Francisco: Jossey-Bass.

Lawler, E. E., D. Ulrich, J. Fitz-enz, and J. Madden. 2004. *Human resources business process outsourcing.* San Francisco: Jossey-Bass.

Lawler, E. E., and C. G. Worley. 2006. *Built to change: How to achieve sustained organizational effectiveness.* San Francisco: Jossey-Bass.

Leonard-Barton, D. 1995. *Wellsprings of knowledge: Building and sustaining the sources of innovation.* Boston: Harvard Business School Press.

Lev, B. 2001. *Intangibles: Management, measurement, and reporting.* Washington, D.C.: Brookings Institute.

Mohrman, A. M., J. R. Galbraith, E. E. Lawler, and associates. 1998. *Tomorrow's organization: Crafting winning capabilities in a dynamic world.* San Francisco: Jossey-Bass.

Mohrman, S. A., S. G. Cohen, and A. M. Mohrman Jr. 1995. *Designing team-based organizations.* San Francisco: Jossey-Bass.

Mohrman, S. A., D. Finegold, and J. Klein. 2002. Designing the knowledge enterprise: Beyond programs and tools. *Organization Dynamics* 31 (2):134–50.

Mohrman, S. A., E. E. Lawler, and G. C. McMahan. 1996. *New directions for the human resources organization.* Los Angeles: Center for Effective Organizations.

O'Toole, J., and E. E. Lawler. 2006. *The new American workplace.* New York: Palgrave Macmillan.

Society for Human Resource Management. 1998. *Human resources management.* 1998 SHRM/CCH Study. Chicago: Commerce Clearing House.

Ulrich, D. 1997. *Human resources champions.* Boston: Harvard Business School Press.

Ulrich, D., and W. Brockbank. 2005. *The HR value proposition.* Boston: Harvard Business School Press.

Ulrich, D., W. Brockbank, D. Johnson, K. Sandholtz, and J. Younger. 2008. *HR competencies: Mastery at the intersection of people and business.* Alexandria, Va.: Society for Human Resource Management.

Ulrich, D., M. R. Losey, and G. Lake, eds. 1997. *Tomorrow's HR management.* New York: John Wiley & Sons.

APPENDIX A

The Practice of Human Resource Management:
A Survey of the Changing Human Resource Function

HR Item Report (*N* = 106)

THIS SECTION ASKS QUESTIONS ABOUT YOUR COMPANY AND THE HR ORGANIZATION.

1. How many employees are in your company? — **32,284 (avg)**

2. How many full-time-equivalent employees (FTE's, exempt, and non-exempt) are part of the HR function? (This number should include both centralized and decentralized staff.) — **909 (avg)**

3. Of the professional/managerial employees in HR, what percentage are in roles that directly support a business unit (for example, generalists)? — **46.2%**

4. Of your professional/managerial HR employees, what percentage are centralized (such as corporate staff)? — **40.4%**

5. What is the background of the current head of HR? (Please check one response.)

   ❑ 1. Human resource management — **74.5%**

   ❑ 2. Other function(s), which one(s)? — **25.5%**

6. Which of the following best describes your company? (please check one response):

   ❑ 1. Single integrated business. — **23.6%**

   ❑ 2. Multiple related businesses with corporate functions providing some integrative support. — **43.4%**

   ❑ 3. Several sectors or groups of business units with some corporate functions and support. — **30.2%**

   ❑ 4. Multiple unrelated businesses managed independently in a "holding company" fashion. — **2.8%**

   ❑ 5. Other (please specify) _____ — **0%**

7.	To what extent do the following approaches describe how your organization is managed?	Little or No Extent	Some Extent	Moderate Extent	Great Extent	Very Great Extent	Mean
	Bureaucratic (hierarchical structure, tight job descriptions, top-down decision making)	20.2	24.0	28.8	23.1	3.8	**2.66**
	Low-cost operator (low wages, minimum benefits, focus on cost reduction and controls)	38.1	33.3	16.2	8.6	3.8	**2.07**
	High involvement (flat structure, participative decisions, commitment to employee development and careers)	8.5	22.6	33.0	28.3	7.5	**3.04**
	Global competitor (complex, interesting work, hire best talent, low commitment to employee development and careers)	21.2	28.8	31.7	10.6	7.7	**2.55**

THIS SECTION ASKS QUESTIONS ABOUT STRATEGIC INITIATIVES IN YOUR COMPANY.

8.	To what extent is each of the following strategic initiatives present in your organization?	Little or No Extent	Some Extent	Moderate Extent	Great Extent	Very Great Extent	Mean
	Building a global presence	24.5	14.2	12.3	23.6	25.5	**3.11**
	Partnering/networking with other companies	9.5	32.4	35.2	18.1	4.8	**2.76**
	Quality	0.9	5.7	22.6	35.8	34.9	**3.98**
	Cycle time reduction	7.5	17.0	30.2	30.2	15.1	**3.28**
	Accelerating new product innovation	6.6	23.6	19.8	24.5	25.5	**3.39**
	Acquisitions	5.7	27.4	27.4	22.6	17.0	**3.18**
	Process automation/Information technology	2.8	17.0	29.2	34.0	17.0	**3.45**
	Customer focus	0	0.9	13.2	27.4	58.5	**4.43**
	Technology leadership	6.6	22.6	32.1	24.5	14.2	**3.17**
	Reducing the number of businesses you are in	57.5	23.6	8.5	6.6	3.8	**1.75**
	Talent—being an Employer of Choice	3.8	13.2	26.4	31.1	25.5	**3.61**
	Cost leadership	5.7	25.5	31.1	28.3	9.4	**3.10**
	Expansion into new markets	5.7	15.2	32.4	31.4	15.2	**3.35**
	Total Quality Management/Six Sigma	33.0	20.8	19.8	20.8	5.7	**2.45**
	Employee involvement	4.8	20.0	37.1	30.5	7.6	**3.16**
	Knowledge/intellectual capital management	6.6	25.5	32.1	27.4	8.5	**3.06**
	Sustainability	5.7	5.7	32.1	35.8	20.8	**3.60**
	Innovation	1.9	16.0	27.4	31.1	23.6	**3.58**

THIS SECTION ASKS QUESTIONS ABOUT
THE HUMAN RESOURCE FUNCTION IN YOUR COMPANY.

---

9. For each of the following HR roles, please estimate the percentage of time your HR function spends performing these roles. Percentages should add to 100% for each column:

	Currently	5–7 Years Ago
a. Maintaining records (collect, track, and maintain data on employees)	**15.8%**	**26.3%**
b. Auditing/Controlling (ensure compliance with internal operations, regulations, and legal and union requirements)	**11.6%**	**15.2%**
c. Providing human resource services (assist with implementation and administration of HR practices)	**27.8%**	**33.0%**
d. Developing human resource systems and practices (develop new HR systems and practices)	**19.2%**	**13.5%**
e. Strategic business partnering (member of the management team; involved with strategic HR planning, organization design, and strategic change)	**25.6%**	**12.1%**
Total	**100%**	**100%**

10. Which of the following best describes the relationship between the Human Resource function and the business strategy of your corporation? (Please check one response.)

❏ 1. Human Resource plays no role in business strategy **5.7%**

(if checked, go to Question 12).

❏ 2. Human Resource is involved in implementing the business strategy. **17.0%**

❏ 3. Human Resource provides input to the business strategy and helps implement it once it has been developed. **45.3%**

❏ 4. Human Resource is a full partner in developing and implementing the business strategy. **32.1%**

Answer Question 11 only if you checked 2, 3, or 4 for Question 10 above.

Please respond to the following questions by circling one number in each row.

11.

With respect to strategy, to what extent does the HR function . . . ?	Little or No Extent	Some Extent	Moderate Extent	Great Extent	Very Great Extent	Mean
Help identify or design strategy options	10.0	21.0	37.0	25.0	7.0	**2.98**
Help decide among the best strategy options	5.0	19.0	39.0	33.0	4.0	**3.12**
Help plan the implementation of strategy	2.0	6.0	23.0	48.0	21.0	**3.80**
Help identify new business opportunities	27.0	39.0	24.0	10.0	0	**2.17**
Assess the organization's readiness to implement strategies	5.1	16.2	25.3	34.3	19.2	**3.46**
Help design the organization structure to implement strategy	1.0	15.2	17.2	29.3	37.4	**3.87**
Assess possible merger, acquisition, or divestiture strategies	13.0	26.0	19.0	31.0	11.0	**3.01**
Work with the corporate board on business strategy	15.0	24.0	29.0	25.0	7.0	**2.85**
Recruit and develop talent	0	2.0	4.0	26.0	68.0	**4.60**

12. Your Company's HR Organization

   a. To what extent do each of the following describe the way your HR organization currently operates?

   b. To what extent is each a part of your organization's HR strategy for the future?

	A. To what extent do each of the following describe the way your HR organization currently operates?						B. To what extent is each a part of your organization's HR strategy for the future?			
	Little or No Extent	Some Extent	Moderate Extent	Great Extent	Very Great Extent	Mean	Not in our Plans	Possible Focus	An Important Future Focus	Mean
Administrative processing is centralized in shared services units.	3.8	19.0	19.0	36.2	21.9	**3.53**	11.4	33.3	55.2	**2.44**
Transactional HR work is outsourced.	23.6	38.7	23.6	6.6	7.5	**2.36**	21.0	44.8	34.3	**2.13**
Centers of excellence provide specialized expertise.	9.5	9.5	27.6	34.3	19.0	**3.44**	7.6	31.4	61.0	**2.53**
Decentralized HR generalists support business units.	10.4	8.5	14.2	33.0	34.0	**3.72**	12.4	32.4	55.2	**2.43**
HR teams provide service and support the business.	3.8	9.5	22.9	40.0	23.8	**3.70**	11.4	22.9	65.7	**2.54**
People rotate *within* HR.	17.0	28.3	30.2	16.0	8.5	**2.71**	7.5	35.8	56.6	**2.49**
People rotate *into* HR.	43.4	41.5	14.2	0.9	0	**1.73**	24.5	50.9	24.5	**2.00**
People rotate *out* of HR to other functions.	45.3	34.0	17.0	3.8	0	**1.79**	28.3	47.2	24.5	**1.96**
Senior HR positions are hired from the outside.	15.1	17.0	23.6	25.5	18.9	**3.16**	23.6	54.7	21.7	**1.98**
HR systems and policies are developed through joint line/HR task teams.	3.8	21.7	31.1	32.1	11.3	**3.25**	10.4	31.1	58.5	**2.48**
HR practices vary across business units.	19.8	40.6	17.0	18.9	3.8	**2.46**	53.8	35.8	10.4	**1.57**
There is a very small corporate staff—most HR managers and professionals are out in businesses.	20.8	28.3	28.3	12.3	10.4	**2.63**	28.6	47.6	23.8	**1.95**
Some transactional activities that used to be done by HR are done by employees on a self-service basis.	10.5	25.7	25.7	25.7	12.4	**3.04**	5.7	17.1	77.1	**2.71**
HR "advice" is available online for managers and employees.	20.8	26.4	27.4	17.9	7.5	**2.65**	7.5	34.0	58.5	**2.51**
There is a low HR/employee ratio.	11.3	22.6	28.3	18.9	18.9	**3.11**	16.0	39.6	44.3	**2.28**
Services are low cost.	7.5	25.5	30.2	25.5	11.3	**3.08**	12.3	39.6	48.1	**2.36**
There is a data-based talent strategy.	18.3	29.8	31.7	16.3	3.8	**2.58**	4.8	28.6	66.7	**2.62**
Partner with line in developing business strategy.	11.4	14.3	32.4	33.3	8.6	**3.13**	2.8	26.4	70.8	**2.68**
There is a human capital strategy that is integrated with the business strategy.	8.5	15.1	29.2	32.1	15.1	**3.30**	1.9	10.4	87.7	**2.86**
Provides analytic support for business decision making.	13.2	25.5	34.0	18.9	8.5	**2.84**	4.7	25.5	69.8	**2.65**
Provides HR data to support change management.	9.4	19.8	37.7	22.6	10.4	**3.05**	1.9	29.2	68.9	**2.67**
Drives change management.	10.4	17.9	28.3	31.1	12.3	**3.17**	4.7	23.6	71.7	**2.67**
Makes rigorous data-based decisions about human capital management.	18.9	29.2	30.2	14.2	7.5	**2.62**	1.9	29.2	68.9	**2.67**

13. a. How has the amount of focus or attention to the following HR activities changed over the past 5–7 years as a proportion of the overall Human Resource activity and emphasis?

   b. Have any of these activities been partially or completely outsourced?

	A. Activity and Emphasis?						B. Outsourcing?			
	Greatly Decreased		Stayed the Same		Greatly Increased	Mean	Not At All	Partially	Completely	Mean
Human capital forecasting and planning	0	0	22.6	46.2	31.1	**4.08**	95.3	4.7	0	**1.05**
Compensation	0.9	3.8	24.5	48.1	22.6	**3.88**	64.2	35.8	0	**1.36**
Benefits	0	7.5	30.2	43.4	18.9	**3.74**	14.4	75.0	10.6	**1.96**
Organization development	0	7.5	15.1	45.3	32.1	**4.02**	83.0	16.0	0.9	**1.18**
Organization design	0.9	5.7	36.8	32.1	24.5	**3.74**	93.4	6.6	0	**1.07**
Strategic planning	0	3.8	15.1	46.2	34.9	**4.12**	92.4	7.6	0	**1.08**
Training and education	1.9	8.5	23.6	48.1	17.9	**3.72**	26.4	70.8	2.8	**1.76**
Management development	2.8	4.7	24.5	34.9	33.0	**3.91**	52.8	47.2	0	**1.47**
Union relations	18.4	15.3	43.9	14.3	8.2	**2.79**	90.0	9.0	1.0	**1.11**
HR information systems	1.9	7.5	20.8	43.4	26.4	**3.85**	44.8	48.6	6.7	**1.62**
Performance appraisal	0	2.8	39.6	35.8	21.7	**3.76**	83.0	16.0	0.9	**1.18**
Recruitment	0	3.8	14.3	39.0	42.9	**4.21**	45.3	51.9	2.8	**1.58**
Selection	0	2.8	28.3	36.8	32.1	**3.98**	81.1	18.9	0	**1.19**
Career planning	0.9	8.5	49.1	31.1	10.4	**3.42**	97.2	2.8	0	**1.03**
Legal affairs	0.9	14.2	54.7	24.5	5.7	**3.20**	53.3	41.9	4.8	**1.51**
Employee assistance	0.9	15.1	63.2	18.9	1.9	**3.06**	16.0	39.6	44.3	**2.28**
Competency/Talent assessment	1.9	1.9	19.8	50.0	26.4	**3.97**	70.5	27.6	1.9	**1.31**
Data mining and analysis	1.0	6.7	33.3	42.9	16.2	**3.67**	78.8	21.2	0	**1.21**
HR metrics	0	5.7	23.8	48.6	21.9	**3.87**	88.6	10.5	1.0	**1.12**

14. a. Do you have a multiple-process HR outsourcing contract?

   ❑ Yes   **22.1%**

   ❑ No, *but* seriously considering (if checked, go to Question 15).   **9.6%**

   ❑ No, *not* seriously considering (if checked, go to Question 15).   **68.3%**

   b. Who is your vendor? (ADP, Ceredian, Convergys, EHRO, Fidelity, Hewitt, Mercer, Wage Workers, Spherion)

   c. How long have you had a multiple-process outsourcing contract?

   3.83 years (avg)

   d. Overall, how satisfied are you with your multiple-process outsourcing relationship?

1	2	3	4	5	6	7
(9.1)	(0)	(13.6)	(22.7)	(27.3)	(27.3)	(0)
Very dissatisfied	Somewhat dissatisfied	Dissatisfied	Neither satisfied nor dissatisfied	Satisfied	Somewhat satisfied	Very satisfied

15.	How has the outsourcing of HR services affected the following?	Greatly Decreased		Stayed the Same		Greatly Increased	Don't Know	Mean
	Overall effectiveness of the HR function	1.2	9.5	31.0	52.4	6.0	12.3	3.52
	Ability of HR to be a business partner	0	8.3	31.0	52.4	8.3	11.3	3.61
	Ability of HR to contribute to business strategy	0	3.7	42.7	47.6	6.1	11.3	3.56
	The cost of HR services	0	32.9	40.2	20.7	6.1	12.3	3.00
	The quality of HR services	3.6	15.7	34.9	37.3	8.4	11.3	3.31
	The value HR adds to the organization	0	7.0	36.0	47.7	9.3	8.5	3.59
	Satisfaction of company employees with HR services	1.2	23.8	39.3	26.2	9.5	10.4	3.19
	Satisfaction of HR staff	2.4	19.0	34.5	36.9	7.1	10.4	3.27
	Commitment of HR staff	1.2	14.1	47.1	27.1	10.6	9.4	3.32
	Mining of employee data by HR	0	12.7	60.8	20.3	6.3	15.1	3.20
	Time spent on HR strategy	0	4.8	40.5	50.0	4.8	10.4	3.55
	Use of metrics by HR	1.3	1.3	54.4	38.0	5.1	15.1	3.44
	Time spent on business strategy by HR	0	2.5	43.2	46.9	7.4	12.3	3.59
	Availability of HR metrics	0	9.0	46.2	35.9	9.0	15.1	3.45
	Use of HR analytic models	1.3	7.9	63.2	23.7	3.9	17.9	3.21

16.	In general, how effective do you think the following approaches to HR outsourcing are?	Very Ineffective	Ineffective	Neither	Effective	Very Effective	Mean
	No outsourcing	38.2	33.3	21.6	6.9	0	1.97
	Very limited: only a few transactional services (e.g., payroll)	2.9	20.6	27.5	47.1	2.0	3.25
	Moderate outsourcing to *multiple* vendors	0	11.8	28.4	55.9	3.9	3.52
	Moderate outsourcing to a single vendor	4.0	12.1	36.4	42.4	5.1	3.32
	Substantial outsourcing to *multiple* vendors	8.8	30.4	32.4	26.5	2.0	2.82
	Substantial outsourcing to a single vendor	14.9	27.7	36.6	16.8	4.0	2.67

17. Please check the one statement that best describes the current state of your HR Information System (HRIS):

❑ 1. Completely Integrated HR Information Technology System. **8.7%**

❑ 2. Most processes are information technology based but not fully integrated. **51.5%**

❑ 3. Some HR processes are information technology based. **32.0%**

❑ 4. There is little information technology present in the HR function. **5.8%**

❑ 5. There is no information technology present (if checked, skip to Question 19). **1.9%**

18.	To what extent do you consider your HRIS system to . . .	Little or No Extent	Some Extent	Moderate Extent	Great Extent	Very Great Extent	Mean
	Be effective	8.9	20.8	44.6	21.8	4.0	2.91
	Satisfy your employees	13.9	29.7	40.6	13.9	2.0	2.60
	Improve HR services	10.9	20.8	38.6	25.7	4.0	2.91
	Reduce HR transaction costs	12.9	24.8	31.7	26.7	4.0	2.84
	Alienate employees	44.0	33.0	18.0	2.0	3.0	1.87
	Provide new strategic information	21.8	28.7	32.7	13.9	3.0	2.48
	Support strategic change	22.8	25.7	35.6	13.9	2.0	2.47
	Speed up HR processes	12.9	21.8	26.7	30.7	7.9	2.99
	Reduce the number of employees in HR	26.7	25.7	29.7	12.9	5.0	2.44
	Integrate HR processes (e.g., training, compensation)	27.7	22.8	29.7	15.8	4.0	2.46
	Measure HR's impact on the business	28.7	35.6	18.8	14.9	2.0	2.26
	Improve the human capital decisions of managers outside HR	31.0	22.0	29.0	17.0	1.0	2.35
	Enable analysis of organization's human capital	18.8	27.7	28.7	21.8	3.0	2.62

19.	Does your organization currently . . .	Yes, Have Now	Being Built	Planning For	Not Currently Being Considered	Mean
	Measure the business impact of HR programs and processes?	20.4	31.6	36.7	11.2	2.39
	Collect metrics that measure the cost of HR programs and processes?	39.8	25.5	26.5	8.2	2.03
	Have the capability to conduct cost-benefit analyses (also called utility analyses) of HR programs?	18.4	19.4	39.8	22.4	2.66
	Use HR dashboards or scorecards?	37.8	24.5	27.6	10.2	2.10
	Measure the financial efficiency of HR operations (e.g., cost-per-hire, time-to-fill, training costs?)	50.5	18.2	19.2	12.1	1.93
	Measure the specific effects of HR programs (such as learning from training, motivation from rewards, validity of tests, etc.)?	19.2	21.2	36.4	23.2	2.64
	Benchmark analytics and measures against data from outside organizations (Saratoga, Mercer, Hewitt, etc.)?	48.5	14.1	23.2	14.1	2.03
	Measure the quality of the talent decisions made by non-HR leaders?	10.1	14.1	35.4	40.4	3.06
	Measure the business impact of high versus low performance in jobs?	12.1	12.1	37.4	38.4	3.02

20.	What describes the way you measure the effectiveness of the following HR programs and activities?	Efficiency	Effectiveness	Impact
	(Please check *ALL* that apply) Responses = valid percent checked YES%; Number in parentheses = (freq. checked YES)	The resources used by the program, such as cost per hire	The changes produced by the program, such as learning from training	The business or strategic value produced by the program
	Compensation	❏ 50.9% (54)	❏ 35.8% (38)	❏ 50.9% (54)
	Benefits	❏ 67.9% (72)	❏ 42.5% (45)	❏ 33.0% (35)
	Organization development	❏ 21.7% (23)	❏ 50.0% (53)	❏ 53.8% (57)
	Organization design	❏ 22.6% (24)	❏ 37.7% (40)	❏ 41.5% (44)
	Training/education	❏ 49.1% (52)	❏ 63.2% (67)	❏ 42.5% (45)
	Leader development and succession	❏ 27.4% (29)	❏ 53.8% (57)	❏ 51.9% (55)
	HR information systems	❏ 65.1% (69)	❏ 29.2% (31)	❏ 15.1% (16)
	Performance management	❏ 26.4% (28)	❏ 49.1% (52)	❏ 42.5% (45)
	Recruitment	❏ 66.0% (70)	❏ 47.2% (50)	❏ 36.8% (39)
	Selection	❏ 42.5% (45)	❏ 41.5% (44)	❏ 37.7% (40)
	Career planning	❏ 19.8% (21)	❏ 37.7% (40)	❏ 27.4% (29)
	Affirmative action	❏ 40.6% (43)	❏ 37.7% (40)	❏ 25.5% (27)
	Employee assistance	❏ 54.7% (58)	❏ 34.0% (36)	❏ 9.4% (10)
	Competency/Talent assessment	❏ 19.8% (21)	❏ 51.9% (55)	❏ 39.6% (42)

21.	How effective are the information, measurement, and analysis systems of your organization when it comes to the following?	Very Ineffective	Ineffective	Somewhat Effective	Effective	Very Effective	Mean
	Connecting human capital practices to organizational performance	20.6	24.7	42.3	11.3	1.0	**2.47**
	Making decisions and recommendations that reflect your company's competitive situation	13.4	17.5	44.3	20.6	4.1	**2.85**
	Identifying where talent has the greatest potential for strategic impact	11.3	18.6	39.2	25.8	5.2	**2.95**
	Assessing HR programs before they are implemented—not just after they are operational	12.5	30.2	38.5	14.6	4.2	**2.68**
	Pinpointing HR programs that should be discontinued	14.4	30.9	40.2	10.3	4.1	**2.59**
	Assessing the feasibility of new business strategies	18.9	23.2	45.3	10.5	2.1	**2.54**
	Evaluating the effectiveness of most HR programs and practices	10.3	23.7	45.4	17.5	3.1	**2.79**
	Supporting organizational change efforts	9.3	15.5	39.2	29.9	6.2	**3.08**
	Assessing and improving the HR department operations	7.2	24.7	30.9	33.0	4.1	**3.02**
	Assessing and improving the human capital strategy of the company	9.3	25.8	37.1	24.7	3.1	**2.87**
	Contributing to decisions about business strategy and human capital management	9.4	22.9	36.5	24.0	7.3	**2.97**
	Using logical principles that clearly connect talent to organization success	11.5	27.1	35.4	24.0	2.1	**2.78**
	Using advanced data analysis and statistics	21.6	33.0	28.9	12.4	4.1	**2.44**
	Providing high-quality (complete, timely, accessible) talent measurements	16.7	36.5	34.4	8.3	4.2	**2.47**
	Motivating users to take appropriate action	12.5	34.4	37.5	13.5	2.1	**2.58**

22.	To what extent are these statements true about your organization?	Little or No Extent	Some Extent	Moderate Extent	Great Extent	Very Great Extent	Mean
	We excel at competing for and with talent where it matters most to our strategic success.	6.1	20.4	31.6	35.7	6.1	**3.15**
	Business leaders' decisions that depend on or affect human capital (e.g., layoffs, rewards, etc.) are as rigorous, logical, and strategically relevant as their decisions about resources such as money, technology, and customers.	11.2	26.5	31.6	25.5	5.1	**2.87**
	Business leaders understand and use sound principles when making decisions about						
	1. Motivation	11.2	32.7	34.7	20.4	1.0	**2.67**
	2. Development and learning	8.2	23.5	44.9	22.4	1.0	**2.85**
	3. Labor markets	8.2	36.7	32.7	20.4	2.0	**2.71**
	4. Culture	7.1	26.5	38.8	23.5	4.1	**2.91**
	5. Organizational design	7.1	33.7	37.8	18.4	3.1	**2.77**
	6. Business strategy	2.0	11.2	24.5	51.0	11.2	**3.58**
	7. Finance	1.0	4.1	19.4	42.9	32.7	**4.02**
	8. Marketing	1.0	12.5	35.4	39.6	11.5	**3.48**
	9. Technology	3.1	18.4	40.8	25.5	12.2	**3.26**
	HR leaders identify unique strategy insights by connecting human capital issues to business strategy.	7.1	16.3	41.8	31.6	3.1	**3.07**
	HR leaders have a good understanding about where and why human capital makes the biggest difference in their business.	5.1	17.3	31.6	41.8	4.1	**3.22**
	Business leaders have a good understanding about where and why human capital makes the biggest difference in their business.	8.2	16.3	31.6	36.7	7.1	**3.18**
	HR systems educate business leaders about their talent decisions.	16.3	34.7	31.6	16.3	1.0	**2.51**
	HR adds value by ensuring compliance with rules, laws, and guidelines.	2.0	14.3	25.5	45.9	12.2	**3.52**
	HR adds value by delivering high-quality professional practices and services.	0	10.2	27.6	52.0	10.2	**3.62**
	HR adds value by improving talent decisions inside and outside the HR function.	1.0	11.2	26.5	46.9	14.3	**3.62**

23.	How much does your Corporation's board call on HR for help with the following?	Little or No Extent	Some Extent	Moderate Extent	Great Extent	Very Great Extent	Mean
	Executive compensation	5.2	5.2	6.2	40.2	43.3	4.11
	Addressing strategic readiness	17.5	15.5	39.2	21.6	6.2	2.84
	Executive succession	10.3	6.2	18.6	23.7	41.2	3.79
	Change consulting	24.0	17.7	34.4	16.7	7.3	2.66
	Developing board effectiveness/corporate governance	31.6	21.1	24.2	16.8	6.3	2.45
	Risk assessment	24.2	23.2	31.6	13.7	7.4	2.57
	Information about the condition or capability of the workforce	9.3	17.5	25.8	30.9	16.5	3.28
	Board compensation	21.3	11.7	23.4	28.7	14.9	3.04

24. Regarding the skills and knowledge of your organization's current HR professional/managerial staff:

   a. How *satisfied* are you with current HR professional/managerial staff in each of these areas?

   b. How *important* are these skills to the professional/managerial staff in each of these areas?

	A. How *satisfied* are you with these skills?						B. How *important* are these skills?			
	Very Dissatisfied	Dissatisfied	Neutral	Satisfied	Very Satisfied	Mean	Not Important	Somewhat Important	Very Important	Mean
Team skills	0	14.3	17.3	53.1	15.3	3.69	0	12.4	87.6	2.88
HR technical skills	0	11.3	20.6	50.5	17.5	3.74	1.0	26.8	72.2	2.71
Business understanding	2.0	20.4	29.6	38.8	9.2	3.33	0	7.2	92.8	2.93
Interpersonal skills	1.0	1.0	18.4	54.1	25.5	4.02	0	14.4	85.6	2.86
Cross-functional experience	5.1	34.7	35.7	21.4	3.1	2.83	8.2	51.5	40.2	2.32
Consultation skills	4.1	16.3	29.6	42.9	7.1	3.33	1.0	20.6	78.4	2.77
Coaching and facilitation	1.0	11.2	32.7	40.8	14.3	3.56	1.0	22.7	76.3	2.75
Leadership/management	2.0	12.2	33.7	41.8	10.2	3.46	1.0	15.5	83.5	2.82
Managing contractors and vendors	2.1	13.4	35.1	40.2	9.3	3.41	12.4	58.8	28.9	2.16
Global understanding	6.2	29.9	43.3	19.6	1.0	2.79	18.6	39.2	42.3	2.24
Organization design	4.1	24.5	41.8	27.6	2.0	2.99	3.1	53.6	43.3	2.40
Strategic planning	7.2	25.8	44.3	18.6	4.1	2.87	0	38.1	61.9	2.62
Information technology	11.2	20.4	45.9	16.3	6.1	2.86	9.3	55.7	35.1	2.26
Change management	4.1	20.4	34.7	37.8	3.1	3.15	0	20.6	79.4	2.79
Metrics development	10.2	38.8	31.6	14.3	5.1	2.65	5.2	48.5	46.4	2.41
Data analysis and mining	19.4	39.8	22.4	11.2	7.1	2.47	6.2	48.5	45.4	2.39
Communications	1.0	8.2	27.8	49.5	13.4	3.66	0	19.6	80.4	2.80
Process execution and analysis	2.1	11.3	38.1	41.2	7.2	3.40	2.1	29.2	68.8	2.67

25. What percentage of your company-wide professional/managerial HR staff possesses the necessary skill set for success in today's business environment? (Circle one response.)

1	2	3	4	5	6	7
(0)	(2.0)	(17.3)	(33.7)	(36.7)	(10.2)	(0)
None	Almost None	Some	About Half	Most	Almost All	All
0%	1–20%	21–40%	41–60%	61–80%	81–99%	100%

26. Please rate the activities on a scale of 1 to 10 by circling the appropriate number. If not applicable, circle N/A.

In view of what is needed by your company:

a. How *well* is the HR organization *meeting needs* in each of the areas below?

b. How *important* is it that HR does these well?

Note: Percentages and Mean are computed with N/A (Not Applicable) responses missing.

A. PROVIDING HR SERVICES

		1	2	3	4	5	6	7	8	9	10		N/A	MEAN
a	Not Meeting Needs	0	0	2.1	3.1	4.1	11.3	25.8	28.9	23.7	1.0	All Needs Met	0.9	**7.42**
b	Not Important	1.1	0	1.1	1.1	1.1	7.4	7.4	25.3	24.2	31.6	Very Important	0.9	**8.45**

B. PROVIDING CHANGE CONSULTING SERVICES

		1	2	3	4	5	6	7	8	9	10		N/A	MEAN
a	Not Meeting Needs	2.0	3.1	8.2	7.1	20.4	17.3	19.4	15.3	6.1	1.0	All Needs Met	0	**5.91**
b	Not Important	0	0	0	0	4.2	6.3	12.5	34.4	20.8	21.9	Very Important	0	**8.27**

C. BEING A BUSINESS PARTNER

		1	2	3	4	5	6	7	8	9	10		N/A	MEAN
a	Not Meeting Needs	0	2.0	8.2	6.1	8.2	12.2	19.4	24.5	16.3	3.1	All Needs Met	0	**6.77**
b	Not Important	0	0	0	0	2.1	4.2	3.2	16.8	22.1	51.6	Very Important	0.9	**9.07**

D. IMPROVING DECISIONS ABOUT HUMAN CAPITAL

		1	2	3	4	5	6	7	8	9	10		N/A	MEAN
a	Not Meeting Needs	0	4.1	12.2	9.2	9.2	17.3	18.4	21.4	8.2	0	All Needs Met	0	**6.05**
b	Not Important	0	0	0	0	1.1	1.1	12.6	22.1	24.2	38.9	Very Important	0.9	**8.84**

E. TAILORING HUMAN RESOURCE PRACTICES TO FIT BUSINESS NEEDS

		1	2	3	4	5	6	7	8	9	10		N/A	MEAN
a	Not Meeting Needs	0	1.0	1.0	6.1	14.3	19.4	25.5	18.4	11.2	3.1	All Needs Met	0	**6.74**
b	Not Important	0	0	3.1	1.0	3.1	2.1	15.6	28.1	20.8	26.0	Very Important	0	**8.24**

F. HELPING SHAPE A VIABLE EMPLOYMENT RELATIONSHIP FOR THE FUTURE

		1	2	3	4	5	6	7	8	9	10		N/A	MEAN
a	Not Meeting Needs	1.0	0	5.2	5.2	15.5	14.4	24.7	24.7	7.2	2.1	All Needs Met	0.9	**6.58**
b	Not Important	0	0	0	1.1	5.3	4.3	10.6	27.7	25.5	25.5	Very Important	0.9	**8.37**

G. MANAGING OUTSOURCING

		1	2	3	4	5	6	7	8	9	10		N/A	MEAN
a	Not Meeting Needs	3.3	2.2	5.5	6.6	14.3	19.8	22.0	17.6	8.8	0	All Needs Met	6.6	**6.14**
b	Not Important	3.3	1.1	5.5	4.4	22.0	13.2	9.9	19.8	8.8	12.1	Very Important	4.7	**6.56**

H. OPERATING HR CENTERS OF EXCELLENCE

		1	2	3	4	5	6	7	8	9	10		N/A	MEAN
a	Not Meeting Needs	1.1	1.1	4.3	6.5	10.9	16.3	23.9	21.7	9.8	4.3	All Needs Met	5.7	**6.67**
b	Not Important	0	2.2	1.1	1.1	5.5	7.7	16.5	23.1	25.3	17.6	Very Important	3.8	**7.89**

I. OPERATING HR SHARED SERVICE UNITS

		1	2	3	4	5	6	7	8	9	10		N/A	MEAN
a	Not Meeting Needs	2.3	3.5	3.5	7.0	19.8	16.3	16.3	14.0	11.6	5.8	All Needs Met	11.3	**6.33**
b	Not Important	0	2.4	3.5	3.5	11.8	9.4	12.9	18.8	18.8	18.8	Very Important	9.4	**7.44**

J. HELPING TO DEVELOP BUSINESS STRATEGIES

		1	2	3	4	5	6	7	8	9	10		N/A	MEAN
a	Not Meeting Needs	3.1	5.1	10.2	7.1	12.2	21.4	17.3	17.3	5.1	1.0	All Needs Met	0	**5.79**
b	Not Important	0	0	0	0	5.2	8.3	12.5	21.9	17.7	34.4	Very Important	0	**8.42**

K. BEING AN EMPLOYEE ADVOCATE

		1	2	3	4	5	6	7	8	9	10		N/A	MEAN
a	Not Meeting Needs	0	0	1.0	7.1	11.2	9.2	18.4	25.5	17.3	10.2	All Needs Met	0	**7.34**
b	Not Important	0	1.1	2.1	2.1	12.6	13.7	11.6	22.1	22.1	12.6	Very Important	0	**7.45**

L. ANALYZING HR AND BUSINESS METRICS

		1	2	3	4	5	6	7	8	9	10		N/A	MEAN
a	Not Meeting Needs	4.1	11.2	11.2	14.3	12.2	11.2	17.3	10.2	5.1	3.1	All Needs Met	0	**5.26**
b	Not Important	0	0	0	2.1	2.1	7.3	17.7	28.1	18.8	24.0	Very Important	0	**8.20**

M. WORKING WITH THE CORPORATE BOARD

		1	2	3	4	5	6	7	8	9	10		N/A	MEAN
a	Not Meeting Needs	2.2	4.3	3.3	5.4	15.2	6.5	17.4	20.7	18.5	6.5	All Needs Met	5.7	**6.76**
b	Not Important	3.3	4.4	3.3	4.4	11.1	4.4	12.2	14.4	22.2	20.0	Very Important	4.7	**7.23**

N. OVERALL PERFORMANCE

		1	2	3	4	5	6	7	8	9	10		N/A	MEAN
a	Not Meeting Needs	0	1.0	3.1	6.3	13.5	11.5	30.2	22.9	11.5	0	All Needs Met	0	**6.71**
b	Not Important	0	0	0	0	1.1	2.2	5.4	20.4	22.6	48.4	Very Important	0.9	**9.06**

We need you to do one more thing. Please let us know whom you gave the executive survey to. We will use this information only to follow up with them. We will not report any individual responses.

(1) Name: _____

　　Title: _____

　　Phone: (　　) _____ Email: _____

(2) Name: _____

　　Title: _____

　　Phone: (　　) _____ Email: _____

(3) Name: _____

　　Title: _____

　　Phone: (　　) _____ Email: _____

APPENDIX B

The Practice of Human Resource Management:
A Survey of Executives *Not* in the HR Function

Non-HR Executive Item Report ($N = 41$)

1. Which of the following best describes the relationship between the Human Resource function and the business strategy of your corporation? (Please check one response.)

   ❑ 1. Human Resource plays no role in business strategy (if checked, go to Question 2). **4.9%**

   ❑ 2. Human Resource is involved in implementing the business strategy. **19.5%**

   ❑ 3. Human Resource provides input to the business strategy and helps implement it once it has been developed. **48.8%**

   ❑ 4. Human Resource is a full partner in developing and implementing the business strategy. **26.8%**

Answer Question 1a only if you checked 2, 3, or 4 for Question 1 above.

Please respond to the following questions by circling one number in each row.

1a.

With respect to strategy, to what extent does the HR function . . .	Little or No Extent	Some Extent	Moderate Extent	Great Extent	Very Great Extent	Mean
Help identify or design strategy options?	10.3	41.0	30.8	12.8	5.1	**2.62**
Help decide among the best strategy options?	7.7	35.9	41.0	10.3	5.1	**2.69**
Help plan the implementation of strategy?	2.6	17.9	38.5	33.3	7.7	**3.26**
Help identify new business opportunities?	46.2	35.9	15.4	2.6	0	**1.74**
Assess the organization's readiness to implement strategies?	5.1	17.9	30.8	33.3	12.8	**3.31**
Help design the organization structure to implement strategy?	2.6	12.8	30.8	33.3	20.5	**3.56**
Assess possible merger, acquisition, or divestiture strategies?	23.7	39.5	21.1	7.9	7.9	**2.37**
Work with the corporate board on business strategy?	25.6	30.8	23.1	17.9	2.6	**2.41**
Recruit and develop talent?	0	2.6	20.5	33.3	43.6	**4.18**

2. Skills and knowledge of your organization's current HR professional/managerial staff.

   a. How *satisfied* are you with current HR professional/managerial staff in each of these areas?

   b. How *important* are these skills to the professional/managerial staff in each of these areas?

	A. How *satisfied* are you with these skills?						B. How *important* are these skills?			
	Very Dissatisfied	Dissatisfied	Neutral	Satisfied	Very Satisfied	Mean	Not Important	Somewhat Important	Very Important	Mean
Team skills	0	2.4	7.3	75.6	14.6	**4.02**	2.4	24.4	73.2	**2.71**
HR technical skills	0	2.4	9.8	46.3	41.5	**4.27**	0	7.3	92.7	**2.93**
Business understanding	0	7.3	36.6	48.8	7.3	**3.56**	0	19.5	80.5	**2.80**
Interpersonal skills	0	2.4	7.3	48.8	41.5	**4.29**	0	17.1	82.9	**2.83**
Cross-functional experience	2.4	12.2	56.1	29.3	0	**3.12**	4.9	73.2	22.0	**2.17**
Consultation skills	2.4	2.4	31.7	43.9	19.5	**3.76**	2.4	34.1	63.4	**2.61**
Coaching and facilitation	2.4	2.4	22.0	61.0	12.2	**3.78**	0	26.8	73.2	**2.73**
Leadership/management	2.4	2.4	24.4	63.4	7.3	**3.71**	0	26.8	73.2	**2.73**
Managing contractors and vendors	9.8	2.4	46.3	36.6	4.9	**3.24**	7.3	70.7	22.0	**2.15**
Global understanding	7.3	4.9	53.7	24.4	9.8	**3.24**	14.6	46.3	39.0	**2.24**
Organization design	0	9.8	22.0	53.7	14.6	**3.73**	0	32.5	67.5	**2.68**
Strategic planning	0	12.2	41.5	36.6	9.8	**3.44**	2.5	57.5	40.0	**2.38**
Information technology	0	14.6	58.5	19.5	7.3	**3.20**	14.6	70.7	14.6	**2.00**
Change management	4.9	4.9	43.9	31.7	14.6	**3.46**	2.4	14.6	82.9	**2.80**
Metrics development	2.4	12.2	48.8	34.1	2.4	**3.22**	4.9	46.3	48.8	**2.44**
Data analysis and mining	5.0	2.5	57.5	32.5	2.5	**3.25**	12.5	45.0	42.5	**2.30**
Communications	2.4	7.3	22.0	51.2	17.1	**3.73**	0	12.2	87.8	**2.88**
Process execution and analysis	2.5	7.5	25.0	57.5	7.5	**3.60**	0	53.7	46.3	**2.46**

3. What percentage of your company-wide professional/managerial HR staff possesses the necessary skill set for success in today's business environment? (Circle one response.)

1	2	3	4	5	6	7
(0)	(5.0)	(15.0)	(25.0)	(52.5)	(2.5)	(0)
None	Almost None	Some	About Half	Most	Almost All	All
0%	1–20%	21–40%	41–60%	61–80%	81–99%	100%

4.	To what extent are these statements true about your organization?	Little or No Extent	Some Extent	Moderate Extent	Great Extent	Very Great Extent	Mean
	We excel at competing for and with talent where it matters most to our strategic success.	2.5	20.0	47.5	27.5	2.5	**3.08**
	Business leaders' decisions that depend on or affect human capital (e.g., layoffs, rewards, etc.) are as rigorous, logical, and strategically relevant as their decisions about resources such as money, technology, and customers.	7.5	15.0	30.0	37.5	10.0	**3.28**
	Business leaders understand and use sound principles when making decisions about:						
	1. Motivation	5.0	25.0	35.0	30.0	5.0	**3.05**
	2. Development and learning	5.0	20.0	35.0	37.5	2.5	**3.13**
	3. Labor markets	0	22.5	42.5	35.0	0	**3.13**
	4. Culture	7.5	15.0	42.5	17.5	17.5	**3.23**
	5. Organizational design	7.5	15.0	35.0	40.0	2.5	**3.15**
	6. Business strategy	0	2.5	22.5	70.0	5.0	**3.78**
	7. Finance	0	2.5	10.0	60.0	27.5	**4.13**
	8. Marketing	2.5	12.5	37.5	45.0	2.5	**3.33**
	9. Technology	0	20.0	35.0	35.0	10.0	**3.35**
	HR leaders identify unique strategy insights by connecting human capital issues to business strategy.	7.5	17.5	50.0	22.5	2.5	**2.95**
	HR leaders have a good understanding about where and why human capital makes the biggest difference in their business.	2.5	12.5	30.0	45.0	10.0	**3.48**
	Business leaders have a good understanding about where and why human capital makes the biggest difference in their business.	2.5	5.0	42.5	37.5	12.5	**3.53**
	HR systems educate business leaders about their talent decisions.	15.0	25.0	37.5	17.5	5.0	**2.73**
	HR adds value by ensuring compliance with rules, laws, and guidelines.	0	2.5	27.5	50.0	20.0	**3.88**
	HR adds value by delivering high-quality professional practices and services.	2.5	7.5	27.5	47.5	15.0	**3.65**
	HR adds value by improving talent decisions inside and outside the HR function.	5.0	5.0	37.5	42.5	10.0	**3.48**

5. Please rate the activities on a scale of 1 to 10 by circling the appropriate number. If not applicable, circle N/A.

In view of what is needed by your company:

a. How *well* is the HR organization *meeting needs* in each of the areas below?

b. How *important* is it that HR do these well?

Note: Percentages and Mean are computed with N/A (Not Applicable) responses missing.

A. PROVIDING HR SERVICES

		1	2	3	4	5	6	7	8	9	10		N/A	MEAN
a	Not Meeting Needs	0	0	2.5	0	2.5	12.5	27.5	27.5	20.0	7.5	All Needs Met	0	**7.63**
b	Not Important	0	0	0	0	0	0	7.7	10.3	30.8	51.3	Very Important	0	**9.26**

B. PROVIDING CHANGE CONSULTING SERVICES

		1	2	3	4	5	6	7	8	9	10		N/A	MEAN
a	Not Meeting Needs	2.5	2.5	5.0	10.0	15.0	25.0	15.0	17.5	7.5	0	All Needs Met	2.4	**6.00**
b	Not Important	0	0	2.6	5.1	2.6	2.6	17.9	35.9	23.1	10.3	Very Important	2.4	**7.79**

C. BEING A BUSINESS PARTNER

		1	2	3	4	5	6	7	8	9	10		N/A	MEAN
a	Not Meeting Needs	2.5	0	5.0	2.5	2.5	20.0	17.5	17.5	25.0	7.5	All Needs Met	0	**7.23**
b	Not Important	0	0	0	0	7.7	0	10.3	23.1	17.9	41.0	Very Important	0	**8.67**

D. IMPROVING DECISIONS ABOUT HUMAN CAPITAL

		1	2	3	4	5	6	7	8	9	10		N/A	MEAN
a	Not Meeting Needs	2.5	5.0	2.5	5.0	5.0	12.5	27.5	22.5	15.0	2.5	All Needs Met	0	**6.73**
b	Not Important	0	0	0	0	2.6	2.6	7.7	20.5	38.5	28.2	Very Important	0	**8.74**

E. TAILORING HUMAN RESOURCE PRACTICES TO FIT BUSINESS NEEDS

		1	2	3	4	5	6	7	8	9	10		N/A	MEAN
a	Not Meeting Needs	2.5	2.5	2.5	5.0	0	15.0	35.0	25.0	7.5	5.0	All Needs Met	0	**6.88**
b	Not Important	0	0	0	0	0	0	7.7	38.5	33.3	20.5	Very Important	0	**8.67**

F. HELPING SHAPE A VIABLE EMPLOYMENT RELATIONSHIP FOR THE FUTURE

		1	2	3	4	5	6	7	8	9	10		N/A	MEAN
a	Not Meeting Needs	2.5	0	2.5	10.0	0	17.5	25.0	32.5	10.0	0	All Needs Met	2.4	**6.80**
b	Not Important	0	0	0	0	2.6	7.7	10.3	38.5	23.1	17.9	Very Important	0	**8.26**

G. MANAGING OUTSOURCING

		1	2	3	4	5	6	7	8	9	10		N/A	MEAN
a	Not Meeting Needs	0	5.7	2.9	5.7	20.0	22.9	14.3	17.1	11.4	0	All Needs Met	31.7	**6.20**
b	Not Important	0	0	2.9	8.6	11.4	20.0	11.4	28.6	11.4	5.7	Very Important	29.3	**6.89**

H. OPERATING HR CENTERS OF EXCELLENCE

		1	2	3	4	5	6	7	8	9	10		N/A	MEAN
a	Not Meeting Needs	8.6	0	8.6	8.6	11.4	20.0	17.1	14.3	5.7	5.7	All Needs Met	26.8	**5.89**
b	Not Important	0	2.9	0	0	8.6	22.9	20.0	14.3	25.7	5.7	Very Important	24.4	**7.29**

I. OPERATING HR SHARED SERVICES UNITS

		1	2	3	4	5	6	7	8	9	10		N/A	MEAN
a	Not Meeting Needs	6.5	0	0	3.2	12.9	25.8	25.8	12.9	6.5	6.5	All Needs Met	39.0	**6.45**
b	Not Important	0	3.1	0	0	9.4	12.5	21.9	18.8	31.3	3.1	Very Important	34.1	**7.44**

J. HELPING TO DEVELOP BUSINESS STRATEGIES

		1	2	3	4	5	6	7	8	9	10		N/A	MEAN
a	Not Meeting Needs	5.1	2.6	10.3	5.1	25.6	23.1	7.7	15.4	5.1	0	All Needs Met	7.3	**5.51**
b	Not Important	0	2.6	0	2.6	15.8	2.6	21.1	28.9	21.1	5.3	Very Important	7.3	**7.32**

K. BEING AN EMPLOYEE ADVOCATE

		1	2	3	4	5	6	7	8	9	10		N/A	MEAN
a	Not Meeting Needs	0	2.5	2.5	0	10.0	5.0	17.5	25.0	27.5	10.0	All Needs Met	0	**7.63**
b	Not Important	0	2.6	0	2.6	5.1	5.1	20.5	23.1	28.2	12.8	Very Important	0	**7.82**

L. ANALYZING HR AND BUSINESS METRICS

		1	2	3	4	5	6	7	8	9	10		N/A	MEAN
a	Not Meeting Needs	2.5	0	7.5	0	10.0	47.5	15.0	10.0	7.5	0	All Needs Met	2.4	**6.13**
b	Not Important	0	0	0	0	7.9	7.9	26.3	23.7	23.7	10.5	Very Important	4.9	**7.79**

M. WORKING WITH THE CORPORATE BOARD

		1	2	3	4	5	6	7	8	9	10		N/A	MEAN
a	Not Meeting Needs	13.9	5.6	0	2.8	8.3	8.3	16.7	16.7	16.7	11.1	All Needs Met	17.1	**6.39**
b	Not Important	2.9	8.8	2.9	2.9	5.9	5.9	11.8	23.5	17.6	17.6	Very Important	19.5	**7.12**

N. OVERALL PERFORMANCE

		1	2	3	4	5	6	7	8	9	10		N/A	MEAN
a	Not Meeting Needs	0	0	2.6	5.1	10.3	5.1	33.3	20.5	23.1	0	All Needs Met	0	**7.15**
b	Not Important	0	0	0	0	0	2.6	15.4	20.5	41.0	20.5	Very Important	0	**8.62**

6.	To what extent do the following approaches describe how your organization is managed?	Little or No Extent	Some Extent	Moderate Extent	Great Extent	Very Great Extent	Mean
	Bureaucratic (hierarchical structure, tight job descriptions, top-down decision making)	2.6	30.8	35.9	25.6	5.1	**3.00**
	Low-cost operator (low wages, minimum benefits, focus on cost reduction and controls)	28.2	41.0	12.8	12.8	5.1	**2.26**
	High involvement (flat structure, participative decisions, commitment to employee development and careers)	7.7	17.9	30.8	38.5	5.1	**3.15**
	Global competitor (complex interesting work, hire best talent, low commitment to employee development and careers)	17.9	33.3	30.8	17.9	0	**2.49**

7. Where do you currently work (please select one):

    ❑ 1. General management   **35.9%**

    ❑ 2. Production   **15.4%**

    ❑ 3. Marketing or sales   **28.2%**

    ❑ 4. Finance or accounting   **10.3%**

    ❑ 5. Technical or engineering   **0%**

    ❑ 6. Other: **10.3%**

(HR, Legal, Operations, Senior Management, Strategic Planning)